UNDERSTANDING SOMATIZATION IN THE PRA(
OF CLINICAL NEUROPSYCHOLOGY

GW01045889

OXFORD WORKSHOP SERIES:

AMERICAN ACADEMY OF CLINICAL NEUROPSYCHOLOGY

Series Editors

Greg J. Lamberty, *Editor-in-Chief*
Ida Sue Baron
Richard Kaplan
Sandra Koffler
Jerry Sweet

Volumes in the Series

Ethical Decision Making in Clinical Neuropsychology
Shane S. Bush

Mild Traumatic Brain Injury and Postconcussion Syndrome:
The New Evidence Base for Diagnosis and Treatment
Michael A. McCrea

Understanding Somatization in the Practice of Clinical Neuropsychology
Greg J. Lamberty

■ AMERICAN ACADEMY OF ■
CLINICAL NEUROPSYCHOLOGY

UNDERSTANDING SOMATIZATION
IN THE PRACTICE
OF CLINICAL NEUROPSYCHOLOGY

Greg J. Lamberty

OXFORD WORKSHOP SERIES

OXFORD
UNIVERSITY PRESS

2008

OXFORD
UNIVERSITY PRESS

Oxford University Press, Inc., publishes works that further
Oxford University's objective of excellence
in research, scholarship, and education.

Oxford   New York
Auckland   Cape Town   Dar es Salaam   Hong Kong   Karachi
Kuala Lumpur   Madrid   Melbourne   Mexico City   Nairobi
New Delhi   Shanghai   Taipei   Toronto

With offices in
Argentina   Austria   Brazil   Chile   Czech Republic   France   Greece
Guatemala   Hungary   Italy   Japan   Poland   Portugal   Singapore
South Korea   Switzerland   Thailand   Turkey   Ukraine   Vietnam

Published by Oxford University Press, Inc.
198 Madison Avenue, New York, New York 10016

www.oup.com

Oxford is a registered trademark of Oxford University Press

Library of Congress Cataloging-in-Publication Data
Lamberty, Gregory J.
Understanding somatization in the practice of clinical neuropsychology / Greg J. Lamberty.
p. ; cm.—(Oxford workshop series)
Includes bibliographical references and index.
ISBN 978-0-19-532827-1
1. Somatoform disorders.   2. Clinical neuropsychology.   I. American Academy
of Clinical Neuropsychology.   II. Title.   III. Series.
[DNLM: 1. Somatoform Disorders.   2. Neuropsychology—methods. WM 170 L223u 2008]
RC552.S66L36 2008
616.85'24—dc22   2007028536

Printed in the United States of America
on acid-free paper

To
Shar & RL, who taught me love and work,
and
Annalise & Vincent, who showed me their value

Preface

I have had the pleasure of being the program chair for the first five American Academy of Clinical Neuropsychology annual meeting and workshop programs and have been fortunate to work with the best that clinical neuropsychology has to offer. In the process of trying to put forth a state-of-the-art program, I ran into a long-standing tendency in neuropsychology—an obsessive focus on "science." While I would not argue against the importance of this focus in making us what we are today, the vagaries of my clinical practice often beg for a more "artful" understanding of my patients. The natural conflict between art and science is what stimulated me to further my understanding of somatization and somatizing patients. It is a rare week in my clinical practice when I see only one or two such patients. More typically, there are questions about "medically unexplained symptoms" in more than half of those I see. Those decidedly clinical data suggested to me that our referral sources must believe that neuropsychologists can (1) distinguish between "functional" and "organic" etiologies and (2) do something about or with those patients who fall in the former category. So, my workshop offering and this accompanying book are the result of many years of clinical curiosity and frustration, and a rather condensed study of the fascinating and sometimes vexing literature on somatoform disorders.

The American Academy of Clinical Neuropsychology has gone through some rapid and invigorating growth over the past several years. Our partnership with Oxford University Press in presenting the AACN/OUP Workshop Series is a fine example of our progress and our focus on offering exceptional continuing education programs to practitioners in clinical neuropsychology. Ida Sue Baron, longtime Oxford contributing author and neuropsychology legend-in-the-making, and Joan Bossert, Vice President and Publisher, Brain and Behavioral Sciences at Oxford, hatched the idea of a workshop series based on the content of our AACN programs. Sandy Koffler, AACN Annual Meeting Committee chair, and Jerry Sweet, AACN president, joined the conversation and soon presented the idea to the AACN board of directors. It was enthusiastically endorsed, and the editorial board for the series was completed by Richard Kaplan, Continuing Education Committee chair, and myself as program chair and vice president. All of these people have earned hearty congratulations and my personal thanks for bringing our first set of volumes to fruition.

Once we agreed to the concept, all we needed were a few authors to turn a book around in a matter of months! This was a tremendous challenge, and one that I believe was ably met. Shane Bush seemed a logical choice given what he has already contributed to the field in the way of ethics guides. He came through wonderfully, and ahead of schedule. I was able to cajole Mike McCrea into providing a volume based on his previous AACN workshops on mild traumatic brain injury and concussion, and he naively agreed. The result was also stellar and should be a standard for years to come. I am very grateful to Shane and Mike for getting the series started with their quality volumes. This third volume has required a special combination of naiveté, willingness to bite off more than one could chew, and a stunning lack of fear—I hope readers will find that, with the help of many dedicated friends, family, and colleagues, I have risen to the challenge.

I thank the AACN board of directors for their enthusiasm and hard work for little more than a sense of pride in bringing good things to our membership and our field. I am grateful to Manny Greiffenstein, who provided incisive comments and sage advice on drafts of my manuscript. I am appreciative of his insights and the challenges he put forth. I am also grateful to my friend and colleague James Jones for insights on the psychodynamic end of the spectrum, and his thoughtful review of portions of the manuscript. I am especially grateful to Shelley Reinhardt, who worked with me on this project and to whom I afforded an opportunity to understand the childlike vulnerabilities of the rare "sensitive neuropsychologist" (if I were allowed to use emoticons, I would put one here). We, as a group, are very appreciative of Shelley's efforts, enthusiasm, and guidance. And finally, I thank those very closest to me, my children and Laurie, who helped me through the times when I would truly rather be doing something else, and acted like they didn't even mind very much.

Contents

Introduction

If you are a neuropsychologist who regularly conducts clinical evaluations, you are familiar with somatization and the various somatoform disorders. Whether you feel a sense of competence in working with individuals who present with multiple "medically unexplained symptoms" is another matter, and is the focus of this book. For many neuropsychologists, somatization, as a clinical phenomenon, is a nuisance variable—something to be explained away as marginally relevant (at best) to brain functioning. It is clearly the case that somatization affects patients' reports and experiences of cognitive dysfunction, but such dysfunction is not typically associated with actual brain impairment (Binder, 2005). For some, this is regarded as the end of the neuropsychological story. However, the changing landscape of health care makes it increasingly important for neuropsychologists to become familiar with the management and treatment of difficult patient groups. Therefore, even if you do not provide direct treatment or therapy for patients, your ability to understand the underpinnings of these complex presentations will improve your diagnostic skills and your ability to make appropriate recommendations and referrals.

Somatization disorder and the various somatoform disorders described in the *Diagnostic and Statistical Manual of Mental Disorders* (*DSM-IV*; American Psychiatric Association, 1994) are clinically vexing. Part of the reason for this concerns the wide variability in presentations and definitions of these clinical phenomena. Chapter 2 discusses general nosological issues in detail, but for introductory purposes, a definition of the subject matter of this book is indicated. Throughout this text the terms *somatization, somatoform symptoms,* and *somatizing patient(s)* are used in a generic sense. That is, these terms are not intended to be strictly descriptive of disorders as defined in the *DSM* or other nosological systems, but rather to describe patient presentations that involve (1) the clinical report of multiple somatic complaints that are medically unexplained and (2) significant functional impairment or disruption in everyday life. There are many other variables to be considered, and that is the purpose of this book.

Somatizing patients can challenge the clinical acumen, patience, and empathy of the neuropsychologist at any stage of the evaluation process and will often do so in the name of asserting their "patient's rights." As a result, the entire assessment process is rife with opportunities to become ensnared in a contentious struggle and to lose sight of the goal of helping the patient. For example, it is not unusual for the somatizing patient to attempt contact with the neuropsychologist in advance of the evaluation appointment. The discussion will typically take the form of questions about a provider's credentials and the test selection or demands for certain accommodations. During the interview and subsequent assessment, the patient may attempt to dictate the course of the interview, bemoan improper treatment provided by other professionals, and directly challenge the clinical choices of the neuropsychologist or psychometrist. For many providers, the most difficult part of the evaluation process is the feedback session. The patient with medically unexplained symptoms will often anticipate a "negative" (i.e., normal) outcome and in the meeting will labor to show neuropsychologists how and why they are wrong, attempt to convince them to change their opinion, or make vaguely threatening comments suggesting incompetence or unethical practice.

With these potential conflicts, it is no surprise that the somatizing patient is often regarded as the bane of health care practitioners. Of course, patients with somatoform symptoms can present in extremely variable ways, from individuals with mild and transient symptoms to those who have virtually made a career out of acquiring numerous diagnoses, evaluation consultations, referrals for all manner of treatment modalities, and even multiple surgical procedures.

While somatizing patients can present a challenge for the neuropsychologist, they can be even more troublesome for the primary care providers who serve as gatekeepers for the numerous services to which these patients feel entitled. Even the most tolerant primary care providers may eventually throw up their hands and beg for help. This is the point at which the somatizing patient is often referred to a neuropsychologist.

Given the small likelihood of actual brain impairment, some might ask if it is necessary for a somatizing patient to be referred for neuropsychological evaluation. The reality is that sorting through cases in which there is documented medical pathology (e.g., in some autoimmune disorders) and cases in which patients present a convincing argument for cognitive dysfunction with nothing more than an Internet connection or advocacy group brochures, can be very difficult and time-consuming in the context of a typical primary care office visit.

Neuropsychologists are uniquely suited to rule out cognitive impairment and to thoroughly assess personality and psychopathology issues that may help to identify the nature of a patient's complaints. As such, they can provide a starting point for a more constructive and reasonable relationship between the somatizing patients and their various providers—if handled appropriately!

For most neuropsychologists, the approach to the somatizing patient falls somewhere between outright antagonism and refusal to evaluate and, at the other end of the spectrum, constructive engagement and progress in moving the patient toward a more healthy and realistic way of life. The purpose of this book is to provide practitioners with the *conceptual understanding* and the *clinical tools* needed to put the constructive approach into practice. Neuropsychologists are encouraged to look upon these difficult patients as an opportunity to employ their unique skills in assessment, case conceptualization, and education/intervention. With the current focus on "best practices" and cost-effective treatments, improving the management of notoriously highly utilizing patients could be a decided boon to our field and to health care in general. Thus, this book is not about the neuropsychology of somatization or the somatizing patient per se, but about effectively identifying, assessing, educating, and referring such patients for appropriate management and intervention.

Chapters 1–4 pinpoint key historical, nosological, epidemiological, and developmental considerations and provide a foundation for conceptualizing somatizing patients, their psychosocial backgrounds, and their needs, both real and perceived. To a greater extent than many health care practitioners, neuropsychologists have the luxury of a more extensive block of time to spend with patients. This affords us an opportunity to listen and interact with patients in a more thoughtful and relaxed way, a distinct advantage over most of the professionals with whom we work.

Unfortunately, once a neuropsychologist has made a judgment that a patient is somatizing—and this can occur even before the patient arrives for the consultation visit—some neuropsychologists limit or avoid consideration of somatizing patients' complex background. This avoidance may serve to limit headaches for the neuropsychologist in the short term, but it perpetuates a problem that somatizing patients encounter with a wide range of health care practitioners.

Chapters 5–7 focus on our current state of knowledge about the neuropsychological assessment of somatizing patients, medical and neuropsychiatric comorbidities, and treatment approaches that are increasingly being shown to help in the management of these challenging patients.

Neuropsychologists are often afflicted with a strong "need to know." Often our response is to collect huge files of data that we massage into standard scores and definitive statements about impairment, abnormality, and effort, or the lack thereof. We try to convince ourselves that we have captured the essence of a complex situation when, in the clinical reality, we are far from the truth. For a variety of reasons—some altruistic and others probably not—there has been an upsurge of interest among patients and providers alike in finding more effective and efficient ways to manage somatizing patients. Through an enhanced understanding of somatizing patients, neuropsychologists can join these efforts by making more appropriate and helpful referrals.

Continuing Education Credit

To access the book's Continuing Education component, visit **http://theaacn.org/continuing_education/**.

Author's Workshop Materials

To download materials from the author's workshop presentation, such as PowerPoints, visit **www.oup.com/us/companion.websites/9780195328271**

UNDERSTANDING SOMATIZATION IN THE PRACTICE OF CLINICAL NEUROPSYCHOLOGY

I

A Concise History of Somatoform Symptoms and Disorders

Somatization and somatoform symptoms have been observed throughout the course of recorded history (Trimble, 2004). Four thousand years ago, the Egyptians proffered theories about somatization that included the well-known description of the "wandering uterus" and its effects on a woman as it moved about her body. So powerful and evocative was that description that it maintained currency well into the early part of the twentieth century. The Greek physician Hippocrates, upon whose musings and thoughts modern medicine was built, did little to alter the concept of the wandering uterus except to provide a name that survives to the present: *hysteria*. In the second century, Galen updated the concept by explaining that hysteria was common in sexually deprived women and recommended intercourse for those females who were married, marriage for the single woman, and "massage" by a mid-wife or physician as a last resort (Maines, 1999). Galen noted that although these measures would prevent the uterus from wandering, the cause of the problem—the uterus—would continue to reside in women, and hysteria would remain an affliction of women only.

As medicine has evolved, so has hysteria. Historian Edward Shorter (1992) notes that in their wish to be taken seriously, patients do their best to present with symptoms that are compelling within the prevailing medical culture. Thus, it is not surprising that the nature of somatoform symptoms has changed in remarkable ways over the years. In the eighteenth and nineteenth centuries, medical science was unable to distinguish between paralysis caused by physical illness and that of a psychogenic nature. As medicine became more adept at assessing symptoms such as paralysis, other symptoms that were not yet easily distinguished came to the fore as part of the next mysterious and difficult-to-diagnose medical syndrome. Shorter (1992) gives numerous examples of symptoms and syndromes that took prominence at one time or another, as their predecessors were rooted out as likely related to mental illness or "functional" causes. The dynamic of wishing to be taken seriously is central to somatization: Unless the symptoms are realistic and suggestive of the possibility of a physical illness, the patient can too readily be dismissed as hysterical or perhaps as a malingerer. Clinically, this is frustrating, but conceptually, it makes sense, of course.

Between the time of Galen and the present, theories about hysteria or somatoform symptoms have become progressively more neurologically oriented and less frankly misogynistic. Although universal agreement about the genesis of somatization eludes us, we have at least progressed to a point where scientific and clinical methodologies allow for more focused study. Chapter 4 discusses some of these ideas in greater detail.

In the Middle Ages, medical conceptualizations of hysteria began to move away from the uterus toward the nervous system. During the Renaissance, British physician Thomas Sydenham (1624–1689), often referred to as the "English Hippocrates," emphasized observation over the theorizing that had characterized medicine in the past (Dewhurst, 1966). Sydenham was credited with observing that hysteria exists not only in women but also in men (in whom he referred to the phenomenon as *hypochondriasis*). He recognized the chronicity of the condition and that people with hysteria had certain personality features in common. Sydenham concluded that hysteria was a product of the "mind," which was obviously a departure from earlier theories (Trimble, 2004).

In 1765, Robert Whytt (1714–1766), a Scottish physician and professor of medicine at the University of Edinburgh, published a treatise on nervous diseases that was important for connecting notions about spinal reflexes and clinical presentations of hysteria and other "nervous" conditions. Whytt's observation of spinal reflexes in lower animals was important in elucidating the broader nature of reflexes in the nervous system. As such, the mind could cause a wide range of different problems in cases where "nerves" were weak or delicate. Shorter (1992) notes that while Whytt's theories were not technically correct, the idea of irritated nerves causing clinical symptoms such as headaches, gastrointestinal disturbances, and vomiting was persuasive and was quickly seized upon by the medical community at large. Thus, from the late 1700s through the Victorian era, a host of unusual and vexing symptom presentations were attributed to problems with nerves. Importantly, "nerves" seemed to enjoy the status of a medical affliction and, at least for a brief time, provided those with somatoform symptoms a ticket to all manner of treatments aimed at calming or healing the nerves.

In the middle of this era, Paul Briquet (1859) produced what was regarded as the definitive monograph on hysteria. Briquet was a French psychiatrist working in the Pitié -Salpêtrière Hospital in Paris, where he collected data on more than 400 hysterical patients from 1849 through 1859. His observations were thought to represent the most extensive data collected on such patients in the nineteenth century (Shorter, 1992). Modern-day efforts to characterize somatization disorder paid homage to Briquet with the eponym *Briquet's syndrome*. The term was referenced as recently as the third edition of the *Diagnostic and Statistical Manual of Mental Disorders* (*DSM-III*; American Psychiatric Association, 1980). In the *DSM-IV*, the American Psychiatric Association (1994) removed the reference to Briquet's syndrome and replaced it with the more generic term *somatization disorder*. Like Sydenham and others before him, Briquet insisted that hysteria existed in men, that it was related to a nervous condition, and that there were many predisposing factors.

The contemporary medical establishment focused serious attention on nervous afflictions in the form of now seemingly archaic methods to bring humors into balance, such as bleeding, blistering, and purging (Shorter, 1992). At the same time, in France, a burgeoning spa industry sought to restore jangled nerves with considerably more pleasurable treatments. The popularity of such treatments has not declined over the years despite the absence of scientific review of the "curative" properties of various waters, poultices, and wraps.

In his most influential work, Jean-Martin Charcot (1825–1893), who cast a large shadow in France and Europe, maintained a neurological view of the causation of hysterical symptoms. Charcot is generally regarded as the founder of modern neurology secondary to his work and teaching at the Salpêtrière in Paris. As he became more interested in treating patients with magnetism and hypnotism, however, his views became decidedly more psychological (Trimble, 2004). Charcot's contact with Pierre Janet (1859–1947) and Sigmund Freud (1856–1939) also foreshadowed a dramatic change from neurological conceptions of hysteria to the psychological constructs that became so influential throughout the twentieth century. Despite the ascendancy of psychological views of hysteria, Charcot remained steadfast in his belief that hysteria had clear neurological underpinnings, though methods for demonstrating the neurophysiological basis of hysteria were simply not available at the time. The evolution of ideas about the neurophysiology of emotion and psychiatric disorders continues to be played out and is discussed in greater detail in chapter 4.

Janet was a psychologist and physician whose ideas about hypnosis garnered Charcot's attention and eventually earned him the position of director of the psychological laboratory at the Salpêtrière in 1889. Janet's work with Charcot led to his development of ideas about the connection between subconscious states and earlier traumatic events. Janet's thinking about suggestibility, dissociation, and the subconscious, while still grounded in a belief in neurological predispositions, is widely acknowledged to have predated those popularized by Freud in the late nineteenth and early twentieth centuries. While the source of Freud's ideas about early trauma remains a topic of lively debate, his influence on modern psychiatry and psychopathology is indisputable. Freud's conceptualization of "conversion" as the psychological or mental process by which specific traumatic events and unconscious conflicts present as symbolic physical symptoms became a dominant viewpoint in understanding the nature of hysteria. Even today, conversion disorder retains a place, no matter how arguably, as a diagnostic entity in *DSM-IV*.

In the present day, we continue to struggle, as a society, with defining the nature of medically unexplained symptoms or somatization. As described in chapter 4, many different explanatory models have been put forth. A hopeful view is that we are coming closer to models that allow us to bring mind and body together again in a manner more in tune with clinical reality. Proponents of such a nondualistic view date back to the eighteenth century, though it seemed that limitations in technology made such suppositions more theoretical than realistic. Over the past 20–30 years, advances in imaging technology and cognitive neuroscience have made it more possible to convincingly demonstrate relationships between neurophysiology and behavior/mental illness (Damasio, 1994; Ledoux, 1996; Schore, 1994).

Unfortunately, despite modern-day neuroscientists' elegant and persuasive attempts to convince the public of the inseparability of mind and body, for many people, stigma and shame cling tenaciously to mental illness and psychological difficulties. As long as this prejudice persists, patients will try to remain one step ahead of their doctors when seeking serious consideration for their discomfort. This general sentiment is echoed by Shorter (1992) in the preface of his book, *From Paralysis to Fatigue*:

> By defining certain symptoms as illegitimate, a culture strongly encourages patients not to develop them or to risk being thought

"undeserving" individuals with no real medical problems. Accordingly there is a great pressure on the unconscious mind to produce only legitimate symptoms.

Whether we will be able to break free of this long-standing tendency is unclear at this juncture. Certainly, the goal of improving diagnostic accuracy and subsequent treatment is to limit the negative impact of these misunderstood conditions.

2

Nosology of Somatoform Disorders

The Goals of Psychiatric Diagnosis

There is a clear lack of consensus regarding definitions and nosology in somatoform syndromes, and this is obvious with a cursory review of the clinical literature. Outside of the clinical context, the use of such terms as *hysteria, somatization, somatoform disorders, functional somatic syndromes,* and *medically unexplained symptoms* is even more bewildering for patients and nonmedical personnel. Typically, a diagnosis is a descriptive label used to convey information about the nature and cause of a syndrome, disorder, or disease. A good diagnosis not only should convey descriptive information but also should communicate information about prognosis and treatment/management possibilities.

In thinking about diagnoses and how they ideally work, an oversimplified example using the common medical diagnosis of hypertension is instructive. *Hypertension* is chronically elevated blood pressure. Systolic and diastolic blood pressures above certain levels (measured in millimeters of mercury) are considered indications of high blood pressure. Provided that a diagnosis of hypertension is arrived at through well-recognized methods, various forms of treatment or management are indicated. These might include the use of antihypertensive medication, dietary changes, exercise, and/or lifestyle alterations, or a combination of these treatments. While there are doubtless debates about subtleties of determining at-risk levels, methods of measurement, and therapeutic approaches, the basics of a diagnosis of hypertension seem clear. No such certainty accompanies the diagnosis of somatoform disorders.

Sticky problems of nosology are not unique to psychiatry or psychology, though they are amplified when the underlying basis of clinical complaints is so amorphous—as would seem to be the case in the somatoform disorders. The prospect of proffering a diagnosis from an assortment of vague and often physiologically unrelated symptoms is problematic. A contemporary debate about the appropriateness of the somatoform disorders category began when it was first introduced in the third edition of the *Diagnostic and Statistical Manual of Mental Disorders* (*DSM-III*; American Psychiatric Association, 1980). In the *DSM-III*, the traditional psychodynamic concept of *neurosis* was set aside for a more descriptive and presumably atheoretical scheme. However, there was also more of a dualistic focus on pathology or abnormality, compared to a continuum-based approach typical of psychodynamic theory. Thus, hysteria as a neurotic disorder in *DSM-II* (American Psychiatric Association, 1968) was replaced in *DSM-III* by somatization disorder, which focused on the clinical description of "multiple somatic complaints" to the exclusion of a presumed neurotic etiology. In addition to somatization disorder, several relatively rare and fairly specific syndromes were included, based primarily on the presence of unexplained physical symptoms.

As the *DSM* evolved, the descriptive and pathological approach to mental disorders arguably positioned psychiatry more favorably vis-à-vis traditional medical specialties. For example, schizophrenia, mood, and anxiety disorders have benefited from this descriptive nosological approach because of a more clear sense of these disorders' biological underpinnings. This has allowed biomedical and pharmaceutical research to proceed, with generally positive findings. Somatoform disorders, as conceptualized by the *DSM* system, have suffered a different fate. Because a "real" physical cause is, by definition, lacking, there has not been much movement or interest in identifying therapeutics for these disorders, except as they might overlap with mood or anxiety disorders. The lack of solid theoretical or biological underpinnings for the somatoform disorders, as a group, has led some to encourage the abolition of the category (e.g., Mayou et al., 2005) in favor of a more basically descriptive or "pragmatic" approach (Engel, 2006).

The *DSM-IV* and Somatoform Disorders

The *DSM-IV* (American Psychiatric Association, 1994) is the current standard of psychiatric diagnosis in the United States, and accordingly, clinicians are often required to reference *DSM* codes in their work. Therefore, a working knowledge of the somatoform disorders as described in the *DSM* is important. As mentioned above, the *DSM-III* introduced the somatoform disorders category for which there are no demonstrable organic findings or known physiological mechanisms and for which there is positive evidence, or a strong presumption, that the symptoms are linked to psychological factors or conflicts. (p. 241)

Despite ample sentiment that the *DSM*-based somatoform disorders category has been a diagnostic failure, the ubiquity of the classification system makes it difficult to ignore. In the *DSM-IV*, the somatoform disorders category changed only slightly from that presented in the *DSM-III*, to include undifferentiated somatoform disorder, which is essentially a miscellany diagnosis that subsumes all presentations that involve prominent unexplained physical symptoms that do not meet criteria for the other somatoform disorders.

For the purpose of providing a definition of somatization disorder, the *DSM-IV* diagnostic criteria are briefly summarized here and can be found in their entirety in table 2.1. First, there must be a history of physical complaints beginning before age 30 that occurs over several years and results in seeking treatment and significant social, occupational, or other functional impairment. These general characteristics seek to highlight the chronic nature of the disorder. Second, symptoms from four separate areas must be experienced: four pain symptoms, two gastrointestinal symptoms, one sexual symptom, and one pseudoneurological symptom. Third, "appropriate investigation" must reveal no specific medical condition that would explain the symptoms presented. Fourth, the symptoms are not produced intentionally, so as to distinguish them from factitious disorders and malingering.

The list of symptoms for the *DSM-IV* diagnosis of somatization disorder is similar to that originally presented in the *DSM-III* and modified in the *DSM-III-R* (American Psychiatric Association, 1987). However, there is some divergence in the number and nature of symptoms required for a diagnosis of somatization disorder in the world's other widely used classification system, the 10th revision of the *International Statistical Classification of Diseases and Related Health Problems* (*ICD-10*; World Health Organization, 1992). The *DSM* standard requires more overall symptoms from a larger number of symptom groups (eight symptoms from four symptom groups) than does the *ICD* (six symptoms from two symptom groups). Further, both *DSM* and *ICD* systems have residual or "undifferentiated" categories that require fewer overall symptoms to be reported. Contemporary *DSM* and *ICD* criteria borrow heavily from lists of symptoms that originate from Briquet's (1859) oft-cited monograph on hysteria.

Table 2.1 *DSM-IV* Criteria for Somatization Disorder (American Psychiatric Association, 1994)

A. A history of many physical complaints beginning before age 30 years that occur over a period of several years and result in treatment being sought or significant impairment in social, occupational, or other important areas of functioning.

B. Each of the following criteria must have been met, with individual symptoms occurring at any time during the course of the disturbance:
  (1) Four pain symptoms: a history of pain related to at least four different sites or functions (e.g., head, abdomen, back, joints, extremities, chest, rectum, during menstruation, during sexual intercourse, or during urination)
  (2) Two gastrointestinal symptoms: a history of at least two gastrointestinal symptoms other than pain (e.g., nausea, bloating, vomiting other than during pregnancy, diarrhea, or intolerance of several different foods)
  (3) One sexual symptom: a history of at least one sexual or reproductive symptom other than pain (e.g., sexual indifference, erectile or ejaculatory dysfunction, irregular menses, excessive menstrual bleeding, vomiting throughout pregnancy)
  (4) One pseudoneurological symptom: a history of at least one symptom or deficit suggesting a neurological condition not limited to pain (conversion symptoms such as impaired coordination or balance, paralysis or localized weakness, difficulty swallowing or lump in throat, aphonia, urinary retention, hallucinations, loss of touch or pain sensation, double vision, blindness, deafness, seizures; dissociative symptoms such as amnesia; or loss of consciousness other than fainting)

C. Either (1) or (2):
  (1) After appropriate investigation, each of the symptoms in Criterion B cannot be fully explained by a known general medical condition or the direct effects of a substance (e.g., a drug of abuse, a medication)
  (2) When there is a related general medical condition, the physical complaints or resulting social or occupational impairment are in excess of what would be expected from the history, physical examination, or laboratory findings

D. The symptoms are not intentionally produced or feigned (as in Factitious Disorder or Malingering).

Perley and Guze (1962) and Feighner et al. (1972) developed symptom lists that included both physical and psychologically oriented symptoms of hysteria. The psychological and emotionally oriented items were eventually removed to provide a strictly physical and presumably more objective set of symptoms for what would become the criteria for somatization disorder in the *DSM-III*. A comparison of these various symptoms and criteria is nicely summarized in Woolfolk and Allen (2007).

I now set aside, for the moment, issues regarding the ability to distinguish between somatoform disorders, factitious disorder, and malingering, as briefly alluded to above. In clinical neuropsychology, this distinction is very important, particularly in forensic evaluation contexts. This issue is discussed in greater detail in chapter 5. However, to presage that discussion, one of the major concerns about diagnostic criteria for somatoform disorders relates to clinicians' (in)ability to determine motivation or consciousness in terms of patients' awareness of the nature of their symptoms.

Validity and Utility of Somatoform Disorder Diagnoses

One might reasonably wonder if the selection of various subgroupings of symptoms within the major diagnostic systems has a basis in validity. That is, do the different diagnostic schemes for somatoform disorders result in a better (or different) characterization of specific patient groups? The short answer is, basically, no (Gureje & Simon, 1999; Liu, Clark, & Eaton, 1997; Simon & Gureje, 1999). Factor analytic studies have identified a basic factor structure that captures the *chronic* nature of *unexplained symptoms* that seems to be true regardless of the diagnostic scheme (Liu et al., 1997). Beyond that basic description, there appears to be a fair amount of variability in individual symptom report from one point in time to the next (Lieb et al., 2002), as well as in the consistency (accuracy) of the report of lifetime symptoms (Gureje & Simon, 1999; Simon & Gureje, 1999). Thus, while specific criteria do not seem to influence the basic description of somatizing patient groups, they may well influence epidemiological estimates of different somatoform syndromes. This observation highlights the fact that current diagnostic criteria are heuristically valuable but quite limited from a practical clinical standpoint. Epidemiology is discussed in chapter 3, but for the purposes of the discussion here, the clinical relevance of the various criteria is that they describe a longstanding pattern of unexplained physical symptoms that can be quite variable and influenced by a multitude of factors.

Throughout this book I use the terms *somatization, somatizing patient*, and *somatoform syndromes* in an essentially generic sense. Thus, a patient with a history of somatization, a somatizing patient, or somatoform syndromes all refer to individuals or groups with chronic, unexplained physical symptoms. In other cases, specific somatoform disorders, as described in *DSM-IV* or in other classification schemes, are referenced when there is a clear distinction to be made. When a specific study refers, for example, to *somatoform pain disorder, hypochondriasis, postconcussive syndrome*, or *chronic fatigue syndrome*, this is specifically stated.

It is well beyond the scope of this book to outline the numerous objections to the current *DSM* classification scheme for somatoform disorders. However, concerns about the category echo common themes that criticize the dualistic nature of the diagnoses, problems with patients' acceptance of the diagnoses, lack of ability to exclude physical causes of some symptoms, restrictiveness of the diagnostic criteria, and general problems with reliability and validity as alluded to above (Engel, 2006; Gureje & Simon, 1999; Kirmayer, Groleau, Looper, & Dao, 2004; Kroenke et al. 1997; Lieb et al., 2002; Liu et al., 1997; Mayou et al., 2005; Simon & Gureje, 1999).

Problems with the somatoform disorders category emerged shortly after publication of the *DSM-III*. Initially, a lack of experience with the new diagnostic category was certainly an issue, though as time passed it became clear that criteria for somatization disorder, specifically, and the other somatoform disorders were quite restrictive and made the conditions appear to be rare. Of course, the fact that many patients troubled by physical symptoms did not meet the criteria for a somatoform disorder did not mean that these patients lacked a clinically significant problem. In the mid-1980s the phrase *medically unexplained symptoms* began to emerge in the literature as researchers and clinicians looked for ways to study the sizable population presenting with somatoform issues, despite not meeting the criteria presented in *DSM-III/III-R* (Escobar, Burnam, Karno, Forsythe, & Golding, 1987; Melville, 1987; Slavney & Teitelbaum, 1985). In the atheoretical spirit espoused in the *DSM-III*, researchers and clinicians were taking it upon themselves to redefine the clinical problem in a manner consistent with their experiences in various settings. This approach remains popular today, in fields such as clinical neuropsychology (Binder, 2005). By using the term *medically unexplained symptoms*, researchers and clinicians have, in effect, registered their disapproval with the *DSM* category of somatoform disorders, while taking a more pragmatic approach to examining a significant clinical problem (Engel, 2006). Ironically, this descriptive and atheoretical approach is consistent with the goals described in the *DSM-III*.

Alternatives to Current Diagnostic Criteria

In the spirit of taking a more descriptive approach to clinical problems involving somatization symptoms, some researchers have proposed truncated categories of somatization in order to capture a clinically representative sample that did not meet *DSM-III/III-R/IV* standards. *Abridged somatization* is a term used by Escobar et al. (1987) for a "less restrictive operational definition of the somatizer." Their experience with a large epidemiological catchment area sample suggested that several variables affected the report of somatoform symptoms, including age, gender, ethnic background, and preexisting psychiatric diagnoses. This led Escobar et al. (1987) to recommend criteria of four or more unexplained symptoms for men and six or more such symptoms for women. The result of this less restrictive definition was a marked increase in the presence of somatoform symptoms within a large (3,000+) community sample, from 0.03% to 4.4%. This was frankly more consistent with observations in clinical samples, and the revised criteria resulted in higher levels of abridged somatization among women, older individuals, and some ethnic groups.

Following the publication of *DSM-IV*, Kroenke et al. (1997) noted that diagnostic criteria for somatization disorder continued to be too restrictive. However, the undifferentiated somatoform disorder criteria were thought to be overly inclusive and not necessarily representative of the problem in clinical or community samples. Kroenke et al. (1997) employed a criterion that was even less restrictive than those used by Escobar et al. (1987): only three or more medically unexplained symptoms, regardless of gender. They added a two or more year history of somatization symptoms as part of their criteria. Kroenke et al. (1997) used the term *multisomatoform disorder* to describe these patients, who were drawn from a large study examining "mental disorders" presenting in primary care settings. Their results suggested that multisomatoform disorder was present in more than 8% of 1,000 patients enrolled in this study. They also found that patients meeting the multisomatoform criteria showed similar impairments in quality of life and more disability and health care utilization compared to mood and anxiety disorder patients.

Obviously, in these two large-scale studies, loosening of what had come to be regarded as unrealistically restrictive diagnostic criteria had a general effect of increasing the number of people described as evidencing significant clinical problems. As such, the ability to estimate the general impact and cost of somatization in the health care environment improved substantially.

Within the realm of somatoform disorders, another prominent focus of study has been a range of disorders focused on different bodily functions or systems that seem to present in different in medical specialty settings. Barsky and Borus (1999) described a number of these *functional somatic syndromes*, which "are characterized more by symptoms, suffering, and disability than by disease specific, demonstrable abnormalities of structure or function" (p. 910). The main distinction between functional somatic syndromes and the somatic syndromes described above is that patients with these syndromes attribute them to very specific causes. Indeed, there is often a self-sustaining culture of patients and health care providers that perpetuate the disabling and serious medical status of these afflictions, contrary to a lack of compelling scientific or medical support. A number of these conditions tend to come and go as a function of public interest or compelling story lines. Examples from over the past 20 years include a range of physical and cognitive problems related to the sick building syndrome, silicone breast implants, electromagnetic fields, and carbonless copy paper, to name a few. Binder (2005) specifically addresses fibromyalgia, chronic fatigue syndrome, multiple chemical sensitivities, and toxic mold and sick building syndrome as examples of functional somatic syndromes that tend to be seen in forensic neuropsychological evaluation contexts. Some from within the medical mainstream acknowledge, however, that there are several syndromes for which clinical medicine has provided some support for basic pathophysiological mechanisms. While the nature of such syndromes continues to be vigorously debated, the most commonly noted such syndromes are fibromyalgia, chronic fatigue syndrome, irritable bowel syndrome, and multiple chemical sensitivities (Barsky & Borus, 1999; Binder, 2005; Engle, 2006; Sharpe & Carson, 2001). It is not the purpose of this book to attempt to resolve the debate regarding the nature of any of these syndromes. However, some have suggested that such "diagnoses" can serve as a means to limit iatrogenic conflicts and complications for patients who find more psychologically oriented descriptions offensive (Mayou et al., 2005; Sharpe & Carson, 2001).

Suggestions for a New Diagnostic Approach

A sizable number of prominent clinicians and researchers within mainstream psychiatry have advocated for adjusting or even abolishing current criteria for somatoform disorders. There is a good deal of overlap in terms of why the category is thought to be problematic. Further, there is considerable replication in the various suggestions offered for "what to do" about this diagnostic category.

For the most part, objections to the somatoform disorders category focus on difficulties with the nonspecific nature of the diagnoses. Accordingly, it is acknowledged that the symptoms composing the various somatoform disorders are diverse and, in many cases, related only by the fact that they are symptoms involving physical discomfort. As a result, the somatoform disorders as described in *DSM-IV* tend to lack diagnostic validity and a sense of coherence (Liu et al., 1997; Phillips, First, & Pincus, 2003; Simon & Gureje, 1999). Mayou et al. (2005) argue for redistribution of the various somatoform disorders among the different axes of the *DSM*. For instance, hypochondriasis could be renamed "health anxiety" and placed within the anxiety disorders category. Conversion would fit more accurately within the dissociative disorders category, and somatization disorder might more accurately be considered a personality disorder with mood and anxiety disorder features. Further, Mayou et al. (2005) suggest that specific symptoms might reasonably be coded on Axis III as "somatic symptoms" or "functional somatic symptoms."

From a practical standpoint, it is clearly the case that somatoform disorders as currently described in the *DSM-IV* simply do not reflect clinical reality for many practitioners. That is, the fairly extensive group of symptoms needed for a diagnosis of somatization disorder gives the illusory sense that this is a rare condition and, consequently, one of little impact. Many studies have indicated that a less extensive level of reported symptomatology is still associated with significant clinical impairment, as well as being associated with a range of neuropsychiatric disorders (Escobar et al., 1987; Kroenke et al., 1997). The *ICD-10* criteria for somatization disorder involve fewer symptoms within fewer categories of symptoms than does the *DSM* and, in fact, seems to be epidemiologically distinct (Woolfolk & Allen, 2007). While it might seem to be a matter of semantics, the fact that patients presenting with even a few somatoform symptoms (as a group) tend to show marked increases in health care utilization is enough to encourage many in clinical and health policy fields to consider changes to the current diagnostic scheme.

The dualistic nature of somatoform disorders is also frequently cited as a problem (Engel, 2006; Kirmayer et al., 2004; Mayou et al., 2005; Sharpe & Carson, 2001). That is, diagnoses within this category basically call for ruling out physical causes for the physical symptoms presented, thus making such symptoms de facto "mental" or "psychogenic." This is an unusual requirement in an era that has reemphasized the clear and strong link between mind and body (Damasio, 1994; Ledoux, 1996), and it further highlights a somewhat inconsistent view of these disorders across different medical professions. Many have argued, in fact, that this "mental" view of somatoform symptomatology has been a significant obstacle to more effective treatment of such symptoms by primary care personnel (Mayou et al., 2005; Sharpe & Carson, 2001; Stone et al., 2002). Ironically, we seem to be building a strong case for the physiological basis of psychological symptoms involved in depression and anxiety disorders while, simultaneously suggesting that certain physical symptoms are solely (merely) psychological. While one might argue that this is based on current findings in the neuropsychiatry literature, such a clear demarcation does not seem fully justified.

Several sources have raised concerns about the fact that somatoform disorders, as defined in *DSM-IV*, are not appreciative of general cultural differences and unique syndromes with which they would appear to conflict (González & Griffith, 1996; Kirmayer, 1996; Kirmayer et al., 2004; Mayou et al., 2005). Some point out the fact that many other cultures do not subscribe to the dualistic system inherent in the *DSM* criteria (Lee, 1997). González and Griffith (1996) note that the *DSM* appears to distinguish between mental disorders that are determined by biology and heredity (e.g., depression, schizophrenia) and those that are more influenced by culture and psychosocial development. These authors contend that the latter kinds of disorders are much more likely to show variability from one culture to another. Certainly, somatoform disorders and dissociative disorders are in this realm. Therefore, it is very difficult to prescribe specific symptoms to characterize a disorder in one culture and have that pertain to another culture with any kind of accuracy or validity. Further, such culturally bound syndromes may not be regarded as pathological or abnormal at all. This view, once again, emphasizes the value of describing behaviors or reporting symptoms, rather than forcing a diagnostic label on an individual when it is unlikely to serve a utilitarian purpose.

Finally, concerns about how patients respond to diagnoses are frequently cited as a major problem with the current *DSM* system (Engel, 2006; Kirmayer et al., 2004; Mayou et al., 2005; Sharpe & Carson, 2001). Clinicians and researchers are concerned about the iatrogenic effects of proffering a diagnosis of somatization, hysteria, or even medically unexplained symptoms because all of these labels tend to carry a strong connotation of "mental illness." The argument is that the very the use of diagnoses that are thought to convey a more objective sense of symptomatology raises the defenses of patients and makes it difficult for them to understand the nature of the problems with which they are struggling. The common experience of patients is that their doctor is suggesting that their symptoms are "all in their head." Of course, this is inherently offensive to many or most patients, and it appears to trivialize their suffering as well as possibly calling their character into question. Whether or not patients' concerns on this level should be considered is likely something that clinicians and researchers will have markedly different views about. It is the case that some practitioners would argue that somatoform symptoms are primarily or even solely psychological and that it is not the job of the clinician to a soft pedal that issue. It seems likely that this occurs more frequently and strictly in evaluative contexts, such as forensic neuropsychology evaluations. In more traditional clinical contexts, the argument is that such labels quite possibly add to patients' somatoform problems and do not get them any closer to understanding the complex nature of their symptom presentations. This broader issue is discussed in detail in chapters 6 and 7.

In summary, the diagnostic scheme for somatoform disorders as outlined in *DSM-IV* has been widely criticized by both clinicians and researchers. As much as having a separate category for these clinical problems has helped, it has arguably caused more confusion. On the positive side, clinicians and researchers have modified the *DSM* criteria in a way that allows a more realistic view of somatoform symptoms as present in the "real world." It seems assured that the somatoform disorders category will receive considerable attention in advance of publication of the *DSM-V*, which is set for 2011.

3

Epidemiology of Somatoform Disorders

Chapter 2 reviews issues of concern regarding definitions of somatization and somatoform disorders. The epidemiology of somatization is obviously tied to the definitions used in clinical and research contexts. Accordingly, there is substantial variability in terms of prevalence estimates of somatization and specific somatoform disorders. Among the lowest prevalence ratings are those found in the actual *DSM-IV* (American Psychiatric Association, 1994). As noted in chapter 2, this likely has to do with the fact that *DSM-IV* somatoform disorders have much more restrictive criteria than those employed by many researchers and clinicians.

As a quick reminder, two basic concepts cited in epidemiological studies are incidence and prevalence. *Incidence* refers to the number of new cases of a disorder or disease within a population during a specified period of time, or the risk of acquiring a particular disorder or disease. Incidence figures are cited frequently in broad epidemiological studies of common health problems such as influenza or chickenpox. The time frame and population under study are important in considering incidence because these allow a more precise characterization of risk. In neuropsychiatric diagnoses, incidence rates are typically low and not really of great interest for our purposes. *Prevalence* refers to the proportion or percentage of individuals within a population affected by particular disorder or disease, within a specific time frame. Thus, we commonly see references to six-month, one-year, or lifetime prevalence (LTP) of a disorder. Prevalence refers to a proportion or percentage of individuals in a particular sample. In this very basic discussion of epidemiology, I refer mainly to prevalence statistics.

Table 3.1 Prevalence Estimates for *DSM-IV* Somatoform Disorders (American Psychiatric Association, 1994).

DSM-IV DIAGNOSIS	PREVALENCE ESTIMATE
Somatization disorder	0.2–2%
Undifferentiated somatoform disorder	Not provided
Conversion disorder	<0.1% to 3%
Pain disorder	"Common" (10–15% work-related disability for back pain alone)
Hypochondriasis	4–9% in general medical practice
Body dysmorphic disorder	"More common than was previously thought"

The generic prevalence statistics cited in the *DSM-IV* suggest that somatization disorder affects 0.2–2% of women and less than 0.2% of men. The *DSM-IV* also suggests that these percentages are variable depending on "whether the interviewer is a physician, on the method of assessment, and on the demographic variables in the sample study." Prevalence statistics for other somatoform disorders in the *DSM-IV* vary widely, from considerably less than 1% to as high as 10–15% for somatoform pain disorder (see table 3.1). The *DSM-IV* is vague in terms of the prevalence estimates, acknowledging the fact that estimates vary widely and depend on many factors. This seems clearly to be the case and has been the focus of many subsequent studies utilizing less restrictive criteria for somatization and somatoform disorder diagnoses (Escobar, Burnam, Karno, Forsythe, & Golding, 1987; Kroenke et al., 1997).

Broad Epidemiological Studies

The National Institutes of Mental Health Epidemiologic Catchment Area (ECA) study (Regier et al., 1984) was the largest to look at the LTP of somatization disorder, in the context of looking at most disorders defined in the *DSM-III*. The ECA used the Diagnostic Interview Schedule (DIS; Robins, Helzer, Croughan, & Ratcliff, 1981), which was developed by National Institute of Mental Health to estimate the LTP of *DSM-III* mental disorders.

Apart from the ECA effort, very few large-scale epidemiological studies were published examining the *DSM-III/III-R* criteria for somatoform disorders. This may have been due to greater interest in more common and better understood disorders such as depression and schizophrenia, though it seems equally likely that researchers and clinicians were not finding the *DSM-III/III-R* criteria effective in characterizing somatoform problems as they presented in clinical settings. Robins and Reiger (1991), summarized data from the ECA, which included more than 20,000 people from five urban settings throughout the United States, and found that the LTP of somatization disorder was 0.13%.

Escobar et al. (1987) employed data from the Los Angeles portion of the ECA study. They found that only 0.03% of 3,132 respondents met criteria for *DSM-III* somatization disorder. However, they found that reducing the number of symptoms required by *DSM-III* criteria provided for a more utilitarian "abridged" somatization diagnosis. Abridged somatization was noted in 4.4% of the study sample—a huge increase that shed light on the fact that somatoform symptoms were common and clinically relevant, even if they were not at the level specified in the *DSM*. Escobar et al. (1987) also noted that there were significant differences in the reporting of somatization symptoms depending upon gender, ethnic background, and preexisting psychiatric diagnoses.

Primary Care Studies

The ability to do a thorough assessment of relatively obscure psychiatric disorders such as somatization in wide-scale epidemiological studies is limited by time and resources. Thus, most meaningful studies on the epidemiology of somatization have emerged from primary care settings. After all, this is the environment in which somatizing patients first present. Longitudinal data from a large international study examining psychological problems in primary health care settings were reported by Gureje, Simon, Ustun, & Goldberg (1997). This study drew from nearly 26,000 patients in 14 countries and reported prevalence estimates between 1% and 3% depending upon whether *DSM* or *ICD-10* criteria were employed. Simon and Gureje (1999) later commented on the fact that the report of medically unexplained symptoms (MUSs) was extremely variable when these patients were followed longitudinally. A striking finding from the follow-up study was that, while overall rates of *DSM-IV* somatization disorder were similar when assessed 12 months later, fewer than half of those initially diagnosed continued to report lifetime symptoms consistent with a somatization diagnosis.

Escobar, Waitzkin, Silver, Gara, & Holman (1998) examined their abridged somatization construct in a university-affiliated primary care clinic using the Composite International Diagnostic Interview (Wittchen et al., 1991). In contrast to the broad general sample noted above, rates of abridged somatization in this sample were around 20%. There were strong associations with various forms of psychopathology and physical disability.

Kroenke et al. (1997) studied a sample of 1,000 patients from four different primary care sites using criteria for what they termed *multisomatoform disorder* (MSD). Like abridged somatization, MSD requires patients to meet less stringent criteria than those from the *DSM-IV*. Patients with three or more MUSs and a two or more year history of somatization were considered to have MSD. Kroenke et al. (1997) utilized a 20-item version of the Short Form General Health Survey (Stewart, Hays, & Ware, 1988) to assess general health-related quality of life. More than 8% of this primary care sample was diagnosed with MSD. Importantly, patients with this diagnosis showed health-related impairments similar to those of patients with mood and anxiety disorders. Further, according to patient reports, there were more disability days and more clinic visits among MSD patients, and greater difficulty in functioning as perceived by clinicians. Kroenke et al. (1997) concluded that MSD is a valid diagnosis and has an independent effect on functional difficulties apart from comorbid psychiatric diagnoses.

In a more recent primary-care–based study of somatization, Barsky, Orav, and Bates (2005) examined self-reported somatoform symptomatology and its association with medical care utilization. In an eligible sample of 1,456 patients, 299 (20.5%) were given a provisional diagnosis of somatization based on the Patient Health Questionnaire (Kroenke, Spitzer, & Williams, 2002) and the Somatic Symptom Inventory (Barsky & Wyshak, 1990). Individuals characterized as "somatizers" were noted to utilize both inpatient and outpatient services at roughly twice the level noted for nonsomatizing patients. This was true for both number of visits and cost for these services. Extrapolating these findings to a national level, Barsky et al. (2005) suggest that the incremental medical care costs associated with somatization alone (i.e., not including comorbid psychiatric illness) is approximately $256 billion a year. Data such as these are certainly persuasive in terms of influencing opinions regarding the importance of more thoroughly understanding and treating somatoform disorders.

Smith et al. (2006) took a somewhat different tack on examining MUSs in a primary care setting. This group used a chart review procedure with HMO patients to identify "high-utilizing MUS patients." This method is distinctive in that it did not rely upon survey instruments administered by nonphysician personnel to arrive at a diagnosis; rather, it looked at a clinical problem based on clinical data. Of 206 patients that were identified, 60.2% had a "non-somatoform diagnosis," meaning that they did not meet criteria for full or abridged somatization based on the *DSM-IV*, but rather had one or more psychiatric diagnoses. Only 4.4% of the selected sample met full *DSM-IV* criteria for a somatoform diagnosis, while 18.9% met criteria for abridged somatization disorder. Overall, only 23.3% of the high-utilizing MUS sample met criteria for full or abridged somatization (somatoform-positive), while 76.7% did not (somatoform-negative). The somatoform-negative group showed less overall anxiety, depression, mental dysfunction, psychosomatic symptoms, and physical dysfunction than did the somatoform-positive group. The implications of this study appear to be that patients who utilize services frequently and report MUSs are not necessarily a homogeneous group. Patients that have MUSs but do not meet criteria for a somatization diagnosis are more likely to be characterized by lower levels of depression and anxiety than by a wide range of psychiatric, functional, and disability issues. In other words, Smith et al. (2006) suggest that all MUSs are not indicative of somatoform disorders and might be better characterized as being somewhere on an "MUS spectrum," with diagnosable *DSM-IV* somatization disorder on one end of the spectrum and somatoform-negative patients on the other (next to normal individuals). This approach is not unlike those discussed in chapter 2 (Mayou, Kirmayer, Simon, Kroenke, & Sharpe, 2005; Engel, 2006) and emphasizes the descriptive nature of proposals for dealing with unexplained physical symptoms.

Neurology Clinic Studies

Apart from primary care and psychiatry settings, neurology clinics and practices tend to see a high concentration of individuals with MUSs as well as symptoms and conditions that are, at least prima facie, neurological. A couple of recent studies have looked at the prevalence of somatoform symptoms in a large neurology clinic and subsequently followed patients with MUSs in a prospective cohort study. Carson et al. (2000) looked at 300 new referrals to a regional neurology clinic in Scotland. Neurologists rated patient's symptoms as a function of the extent to which they were characterized by organic or neurological findings. They used the SF-36 (Ware & Sherbourne, 1992) and the PRIME-MD (Spitzer, Williams, & Kroenke, 1994) health surveys to rate general health status and depressive disorders. Three hundred new patients were included in the study. Neurologists rated the patients' symptoms in terms of how much they were characterized by neurological disease, using the ratings "not at all explained," "somewhat explained," "largely explained," and "completely explained." The percentages associated with these labels were, respectively, 11%, 19%, 27%, and 43%. Thus, 90 of 300 patients (30%) had substantially unexplained symptomatology. Patients with lower "organicity" ratings consistently showed a higher number of median physical symptoms and pain complaints. Further, 70% of patients in the "not at all explained" group had a depression or anxiety disorder, compared to 32% of patients in the "completely explained" group.

A follow-up study by Carson et al. (2003) reported on 66 of the 90 patients who were originally designated as showing significantly unexplained symptoms. Fourteen percent of these patients rated themselves as much or somewhat worse, while 63% reported no change or modest improvement; 23% of the patients were "much better." The best predictor of poor outcome at follow-up was greater physical difficulty at baseline. Fifty-four percent of patients with unexplained symptoms at baseline showed no improvement or worsening symptoms eight months later. In no case did an actual neurological cause emerge as the reason for the originally unexplained symptoms at follow-up.

Fink, Hansen, and Sondergaard (2005) also completed a study with consecutive neurology inpatients and outpatients. They used the Schedules for Clinical Assessment in Neuropsychiatry (World Health Organization, 1998) and modified versions of the Symptom Checklist and the Whiteley Index to assess a range of neuropsychiatric symptoms. In their sample of 198 first-time neurology referrals, 61% of patients had at least one MUS, and 34.9% met diagnostic criteria for *ICD-10* somatoform disorder (with a similar percentage noted for *DSM-IV* criteria). Outpatients were more likely to have a somatoform diagnosis than were inpatients, and women were more likely to have somatoform diagnoses than were men. The gender difference was much more pronounced in younger (18–44 years old) and older (>60 years old) patients, with little gender difference in the middle-age group (45–59). Among patients with somatoform diagnoses, 60.5% also had another psychiatric diagnosis.

Collectively, patients referred to neurology clinics tended to meet criteria for somatoform diagnoses about 30% of the time. Within this patient group, there were more females, more psychiatric diagnoses, and higher levels of physical dysfunction and disability. This is in contrast to primary care settings, in which roughly 20% of patients tend to meet either full or abridged criteria for somatoform disorders. Of course, as a medical specialty, neurologists see a more highly selected sample of patients with physical complaints. Un-explained physical symptoms are presumably one of the reasons a primary care physician might refer to neurology, and so it makes sense that the proportion of patients with somatoform symptoms and diagnoses is higher in the neurology setting. Similar to what is found in primary care settings, individuals with somatoform symptoms and diagnoses in neurology settings consistently show a high level of comorbid psychiatric diagnoses.

Pediatric Somatization

Somatoform symptoms are common in the pediatric clinical setting. However, because of various diagnostic criteria, such as chronicity of symptoms and onset before 30 years of age, most somatoform disorders do not fit with symptom presentations in younger patients. About 10 years ago, Fritz, Fritsch, and Hagino (1997) reviewed literature from the previous 10 years with regard to conceptual and clinical reports of somatization in children. Their basic conclusion, not surprisingly, was that there was a lack of developmentally appropriate schemas, and they called for more thorough outcome studies. Of course, there are many clinical reports of somatoform symptoms in children and adolescents, particularly as they relate to specific disorders or health circumstances. However, it is still not the case that much of a conceptually coherent literature exists in this area.

Campo, Jansen-McWilliams, Comer, and Kelleher (1999) sought to examine a group of pediatric "somatizers" to determine if this group was at risk for greater psychopathology, functional impairment, and utilization of health services. They employed parental reports of pain-related symptomatology to construct a somatization group from a cohort of children 4–15 years of age from a pediatric primary care clinic. Children with and without significant somatization were compared on a number of variables, including demographic, psychopathologic, functional status, and utilization. Campo et al. (1999) found that adolescents were more likely to be classified as somatizers, as were females, minority individuals, children from urban practices, nonintact families, and families with lower parental education. Within these groups, there was also a heightened risk of clinician and parent identified psychopathology, poor school performance, perceived health impairment, and increased utilization. These findings tend to mirror findings from the adult literature in terms of risk factors.

A larger scale Italian study was conducted by Masi, Favilla, Millepiedi, and Mucci (2000). Their interest was in identifying the prevalence of somatic symptoms in children and adolescents who were referred to a pediatric neurology and psychiatry practice for emotional/behavioral disorders. They examined 96 males and 66 females using a structured diagnostic interview. Somatic symptoms were reported in 69.2% of the sample. Headache was the most frequent symptom, reported in 50.6% of the sample. Younger children tended to show higher reporting of abdominal complaints, and there were no gender differences in overall somatic symptom report. Once again, patients with anxiety and depression reported a higher level of somatic symptomatology, particularly headache. Somatic symptoms did not differentiate patients with anxiety versus depression. The authors concluded that somatoform symptoms need to be considered as a possible indication of unidentified psychiatric disorder.

Campo and Fritz (2001) offered some recommendations for managing pediatric somatization based on the scant literature available. Their recommendations drew from the adult literature and emphasize cognitive behavioral approaches along with treatment of psychopathology such as depression and anxiety. It seems clear in the pediatric literature that a conceptual understanding of somatization is even more lacking than it is in the adult literature. Again, the focus has typically been on specific psychiatric disorders and the physical conditions that are often seen as co-occurring with somatoform symptoms. Nonetheless, some of these studies provide glimpses into the development of somatoform profiles and, to the extent that these can identify patients at an earlier age, might prove useful in working with at-risk children and adolescents to decrease the likelihood of adult somatization and somatoform disorders.

Summary

Somatoform diagnoses tend to be fairly uncommon in large-scale epidemiological studies. However, the prevalence of these disorders in more selected primary care and neurology settings increases dramatically, particularly when less stringent criteria are employed. Across a number of different studies, 20–30% of primary care and specialty clinic referrals present with significant somatoform symptoms. Within this broad group, there tend to be higher numbers of women, minorities, and individuals with significant comorbid psychopathology (most often depression and anxiety disorders). Some researchers have emphasized this comorbidity issue and suggest that somatoform disorders are simply a different manifestation of an underlying psychiatric disorder. Others have determined that somatoform symptoms are independently problematic and the cause of significant utilization and health care expense. It is clear that *DSM-IV* definitions of somatoform disorders lack coherence, and this fact makes it difficult to address difficulties and make recommendations for individuals in the somatoform disorder group. Chapter 4 addresses developmental and personality considerations as a means of trying to understand some of the patterns noted in the epidemiological literature.

It is interesting, and perhaps the crux of the matter, that "psychiatric" diagnoses such as somatization or somatoform disorders present so infrequently in psychiatry clinic settings. This is not to say that patients seen in psychiatry settings do not show somatoform symptoms, but rather that patients with clear somatoform disorders do not present for treatment in psychiatry clinic. This should not be surprising because patients with somatoform disorders clearly see their issues as related to physical functioning. Thus, the likelihood that patients present in primary care, neurology, rheumatology, and other medical specialty settings is great. Chapter 2 reviews a number of general recommendations with regard to how to treat somatoform disorders from the nosological perspective. This obviously has bearing on the future of how such patients are conceptualized and treated. There is now a wide-ranging call for rapprochement between primary care, neurology, and psychiatry specialties. For more than a decade, the traditional linkage between mind and body has been reemphasized. Arguably, medical specialties have spent some time ignoring matters of mind and emotion, which has resulted in generally less adequate treatment of the "whole" patient. Ironically, psychiatry's push to become a biologically oriented specialty area has also contributed to the disconnection of mind and body. By conceptualizing psychiatric disorders as primarily biologically based, there has been a tendency to move away from traditional psychodynamic and developmental concepts in trying to understand how emotional factors affect health more generally. This movement was clearly ushered in with the *DSM-III*, which sought to be a descriptive and atheoretical classification system. While this may assist researchers with designing studies to assess the reliability and validity of diagnostic labels, the richness of clinical explanatory models has been minimized.

Chapter 4 discusses a number of developmental, theoretical, and cultural viewpoints as they relate to understanding the nature of somatization and somatoform disorders. Such information needs to be at the foundation of our understanding of patients who present with somatoform symptoms.

4

Etiological Theories of Somatoform Disorders

Despite the fact that diagnostic systems and epidemiologists seek to avoid messy issues of etiology in neuropsychiatric disorders, there is considerable interest in the developmental underpinnings of somatization. There is a wide range of opinion regarding the origins of somatization, some of which have been alluded to in the first several chapters. Among psychiatric disorders, however, somatoform disorders are unique. With most *DSM* diagnostic categories, there is an implicit expectation that the symptoms comprising a given diagnosis have some biological foundation. For example, it is widely believed that depression involves problems with serotonin and norepinephrine availability, and that schizophrenia and bipolar affective disorder relate to abnormalities in the dopaminergic system. In somatization, symptoms "are not fully explained by a general medical condition, by the direct effects of a substance, or by another mental disorder" (American Psychiatric Association, 1994, p. 445). In other words, the symptoms are primarily psychological. The *DSM-IV* acknowledges that somatoform disorders are not grouped together based on a presumed shared etiology, but rather on the need to rule out medical or substance-use–related factors. In other words, they are diagnoses by exclusion. Perhaps the major problem with diagnoses by exclusion is that this often prolongs or increases the number of contacts with specialists and primary care providers. In somatization, persistent doctor shopping is at the heart of the clinical problem, and the notion that an acceptable diagnosis will be found often seems to be the somatizing patient's Holy Grail.

A gauntlet was thrown down in the *DSM-III* in the first sentence of the Somatoform Disorders section:

The essential features of this group of disorders are physical symptoms suggesting physical disorder (hence, Somatoform) for which there are no demonstrable organic findings or known physiological mechanisms and for which there is positive evidence, or a strong presumption, that the symptoms are linked to psychological factors or conflicts. (American Psychiatric Association, 1980, p. 241)

Thus, in most basic terms, symptoms presented by patients were either "demonstrably organic" or "psychological" in nature. This is the dualism frequently referred to in preceding chapters of this book. Of course, there was no specific guidance as to how to make this distinction definitively. The threshold for determining whether or not symptoms are "real" is as different as the backgrounds and biases of a given provider. Some might pronounce a symptom or patient "somatoform" with no more than a brief review of history and a cursory physical examination, while others might order all manner of laboratory tests, imaging studies, and multiple referrals to specialists. In the end, it is often true that both approaches end up with the same result—distressed patients with no clear answers regarding their pain and suffering.

The clinical aspects of this conflict are discussed in more detail in chapters 6 and 7, though it is important to reiterate the basic tension between the psychological and physical aspects of somatization. As noted in chapter 1, the earliest philosophers and physicians were wont to understand things in material (i.e., physical) terms, whereas this tide turned dramatically in the nineteenth century with the work of Freud and others. Today, most clinicians, researchers, and theorists espouse a more synthetic approach with a fundamental acknowledgment of the inseparability of mind and body.

Biologically Oriented Theories of Somatoform Disorders

Comprehensive biologically oriented theories of somatoform disorders are frankly rare. This probably speaks to two issues. First, as frequently noted in preceding chapters, the diagnostic criteria for somatoform disorders simply do not reflect a typical clinical state of affairs. As such, it would be very difficult to develop a comprehensive biologically oriented theory to account for multiple symptoms reported by somatizing patients. The reality is that the symptoms reported do not fit together in a medically or biologically cohesive way, and a theory to make them do so would likely seem as fanciful as the wandering uterus theory of ancient times. Second, the overwhelming evidence showing links to psychological and cultural influences would make any such biologically oriented theory seem limited and naive. Thus, while progress has been made in understanding the specific biologically oriented symptoms seen in various somatoform disorders, the notion that biological and psychological factors cannot be separated is not new. Fenichel (1945) describes the issue succinctly in his classic text, *The Psychoanalytic Theory of Neurosis*:

> The term "psychosomatic" disturbances has the disadvantage of suggesting a dualism that does not exist. Every disease is "psychosomatic"; for no "somatic" disease is entirely free from "psychic" influence—an accident may have occurred for psychogenic reasons, and not only the resistance against infections but all vital functions are continually influenced by the emotional state of the organism—even the most "psychic" conversion may be based on a purely "somatic" compliance. (p. 237)

Despite our current understanding of the psychological nature of somatization, theories about somatoform disorders have been found on different ends of a familiar spectrum (i.e., mind vs. body, nature vs. nurture, biological vs. psychological). These theories differ in terms of how much somatoform symptoms are proposed to relate to biological/constitutional factors on one end of the spectrum and developmental/environmental factors on the other. However, since somatoform disorders, at least as defined since the *DSM-III*, are explicitly without a clear biological cause, theories about somatoform disorders as a group have become less of a focus of researchers. Rather, researchers in neuropsychiatry or psychosomatics have focused on putatively more biologically oriented models of functional somatic syndromes (Barsky & Borus, 1999; Kirmayer, Groleau, Looper, & Dao, 2004; Sharpe & Carson, 2001). Thus, instead of trying to account for the nature and complexity of whole patients with somatoform disorders, reductionistic subgroupings of symptoms, dysfunction in specific bodily systems, and reactions to various environmental toxins have become focal points that have effectively diverted scrutiny from the individual to the "disease."

The biologically oriented theories of the past are much more basic and simplistic than the primarily psychological theories of the nineteenth and twentieth centuries. Identifying basic physical causes of all manner of maladies has always been the task of physicians. While the existence of different mental illnesses had been evident since ancient times, there was a considerable press to identify the constitutional factors causing these problems. Thus, hysteria was considered a product of a wandering uterus, misaligned humors, or a malfunctioning nervous system (Shorter, 1992). These theories are referred to in chapter 2, and I do not review them in detail here because they are mainly of historical interest. Nevertheless, there is something fundamental and seductive about being able to attribute one's struggles to physical illness/injury as opposed to psychological disturbance, and this carries through to the present time.

Current conceptualizations of various functional somatic syndromes (Barsky & Borus, 1999; Nimnuan, Rabe-Hesketh, Wessely, & Hotopf, 2001; Sharpe & Carson, 2001) aim to be more integrative or less dualistic, but the theme of protestation of the "real" physical nature of such disorders as fibromyalgia and chronic fatigue is unmistakable. Examples of this bias abound in various advocacy groups' Web sites (e.g., National Fibromyalgia Association, www.fmaware.org; Chronic Fatigue and Immune Dysfunction Syndrome Association of America, www.cfids.org). While these groups seek to assist patients in many ways, there seems to be a clear bias that validates suffering by applying a medical label to the constellation of symptoms experienced. In contrast, a more balanced and integrative approach is espoused by the International Foundation for Functional Gastrointestinal Disorders (www.aboutibs.org) and the Nonepileptic Seizure Organization (www.non-epilepticseizures.com). These groups seek to educate the public on a range of problems that are distressing, sometimes disabling, and not clearly related to structural brain or CNS abnormalities. As mentioned in chapter 2, use of the term *functional* is a seemingly more palatable way of describing the reality of serious and troubling physical symptoms that are nonetheless not clearly related to structural abnormalities.

Although not a biological theory per se, evolutionary psychology (EP) offers a theoretical framework to understand false illness signaling. EP represents the application of Darwin's theory of natural selection to psychological mechanisms. The hypothetical constructs (unobservable causal mechanisms) of EP are cognitive modules that produce behaviors relevant to either classic fitness (personal survival and reproduction) or inclusive fitness (survival of genetically related kin) (Buss, 1999). EP adherents literally believe that our brains are actually "Stone Age computers" insofar as they evolved to cope with recurrent problems of the Pleistocene age. The modern age, dated from the development of writing, is too brief to have modified the brain through natural selection, a process taking hundreds if not thousands of generations. These cognitive mechanisms weight asymmetrical cost–benefit structure of any behavioral outcomes in fitness currency. Proof that a psychological mechanism is an evolved mechanism includes the rapidity with which a behavior is learned. It is commonly accepted now that the universally rapid language acquisition of children cannot be explained by a "cultural transmission" model (Pinker, 1999).

An EP approach to somatization asks whether false illness signaling represents an innate psychological mechanism triggered by situational exigencies. There is no doubt that somatization is associated with access to resources or has survival value; the question is whether somatization represents a behavioral polymorphism that bestows survival value. Of special interest is the repeated finding of psychopathy or antisocial traits such as substance abuse in male relatives of somatizing females (Guze, 1993; Martin, Cloninger, Guze, & Clayton, 1986). Harpending and Sobus (1987) conjectured that somatization disorder represents a sex-modified phenotypic variant of psychopathy. In an innovative treatise, Linda Mealy (1995) conjectured that somatization represented evidence for secondary psychopathy; females with partial psychopathic traits produce false illness signals to access resources during particularly stressful times. Hence, the theory is that somatization disorder represents a particularly female strategy of signaling false illness to influence others' perception. This does not rule out somatization disorder in men, but the empirical reality is that somatization disorder is significantly overrepresented in females (as noted in chapter 3).

Behaviorally Oriented Theories of Somatoform Disorders

Like biologically oriented theories, behavioral theories of somatization are reductionistic and relatively simple. The ability to focus on variables of interest to the exclusion of all manner of moderating factors (most notably developmental psychopathology) allows leaner research designs and more straightforward statements about results. This is not an indictment of behaviorally oriented models, because this level of analysis is useful in helping us understand the basic nature of behaviors that compose somatization and somatoform disorders. Behavioral models have most widely and consistently been applied to various kinds of pain problems (Fordyce, 1976; Keefe & Gil, 1986; Turk, Meichenbaum, & Genest, 1983). Unlike the other somatoform disorders, pain and pain behaviors are relatively discrete and easily operationalized. That is, most people can identify behaviors that suggest a person is experiencing pain. These would include certain body postures, grimaces or facial expressions, use of medication, and avoidance of work and activity.

Wilbert E. Fordyce was a pioneer in the use of operant conditioning principles in understanding pain and pain behaviors (Fordyce et al., 1973; Fordyce,

1976). In operant behavior therapy, patients are reinforced or rewarded for displaying healthy behaviors, while consequences are placed on pain behaviors such wincing, using medications, avoiding movement, or seeking treatment. The basic operant conditioning paradigm can be applied more broadly to pain and somatoform symptoms in a manner that allows us to conceptualize the production of physical symptoms as operant behavior with a specific goal. That is, pain behaviors or various somatoform symptoms are used to secure reinforcement in the form of attention from loved ones, rest, or time away from work. The connection between some somatoform symptoms and the eventual reinforcement is not always clear, and from a behavioral standpoint, this makes it very difficult to distinguish between somatoform disorders, factitious disorders, and malingering. Some would argue that the notion of volition is essentially irrelevant and that these classes of disorders are functionally the same. That is, in all three kinds of disorders, individuals are exaggerating pain or physical discomfort for a certain effect or to obtain a certain kind of reinforcement the specific nature of which is often very difficult to determine.

In neuropsychology practice, the clinical features of a large group of individuals with mild traumatic brain injuries (mTBI; Larrabee, 2005b) or postconcussive syndrome (Alexander, 1992) are closely allied with both the dynamics of the functional somatic syndromes and pain disorders. As such, mTBI might reasonably be seen as either a biologically oriented disorder or one that is well explained by operant learning principles. On the one hand, mTBI patients are often characterized using a model of physical injury or illness that is employed as a wide-ranging explanatory model for the many symptoms (both specific and nonspecific) reported by affected individuals (Bigler, 2003; Mittenberg & Strauman, 2000). On the other hand, some have suggested that all manner of symptomatology seen in mTBI patients is a classic example of operant behavior. In this regard, the somatoform behaviors put forth by patients with postconcussive syndrome are geared toward securing reinforcement. Of course, it is most likely that some elements of both models operate in the modal mTBI case, at different points in time.

Conveniently, biological and behavioral models do not need to invoke notions of consciousness or volition. However, as mentioned above, this can complicate the diagnostic picture, because current *DSM* notions of somatoform disorders, factitious disorders, and malingering hinge on patients' conscious awareness of the nature of their symptoms. This important distinction is revisited in chapter 6. In both biological and behavioral theories, there is a tendency to eschew messy psychological factors that complicate the basic

Understanding Somatization

nature of our understanding. However, as discussed in chapter 6, the most successful methods for treating somatoform disorders do, in fact, incorporate psychological and emotional factors that are regarded as superfluous complications in these more basic models.

Psychoanalytically Oriented Theories of Somatoform Disorders

Much of our popular understanding of somatization and somatoform disorders has its theoretical genesis in the work of Pierre Janet, Josef Breuer, and Sigmund Freud. Wilhelm Stekel, a Viennese psychoanalyst, coined the term *somatization* to refer to a process whereby a deep-seated neurosis could be expressed through a physical disorder (as cited in Taylor, Bagby, & Parker, 1997, p. 116). Brown (2004) provides a thorough review of psychological mechanisms purported to underlie medically unexplained symptoms. He notes that medically unexplained symptoms have traditionally been based on concepts that became popular in the late nineteenth and early twentieth centuries: dissociation and conversion.

In describing *dissociation*, Janet (1907) proposed that some patients' attention narrows when they are exposed to traumatic events. As a result of this narrowing, individuals will attend to a limited amount of sensory information. Eventually, some sensory information can be neglected if the individual develops a pattern of concentrating on a limited number of symptoms (in the case of conversion, as described further below, on physical symptoms). Over time, the lack of other compelling input causes a person to interpret subjective experiences as actual perceptions. These perceptions are then awakened in an automatic fashion under many different kinds of circumstances. Put more succinctly, dissociative somatizing patients selectively attend to physical symptoms to the exclusion of other perceptions, particularly when they are under stress. These subjective experiences (pain, sensory loss, fatigue, cognitive dysfunction, etc.) become very "real" and result in "unexplained" symptoms. Janet (1907) believed that dissociation was an indication of mental infirmity. That is, only individuals with some kind of constitutional weakness would use dissociation in the manner described. Contemporary theories tend to view dissociative responses on a more continuous basis, which suggests that some dissociation is normal under traumatic conditions and that it is employed to varying degrees depending upon the person and circumstances (Kihlstrom, 1992).

Conversion is a concept that is popularly accepted and developed out of the work of Breuer, Freud, and Strachey (1957). Simply stated, *conversion* refers to the notion that unconscious emotional conflicts are literally converted into various bodily symptoms that are representative of previously experienced trauma or the nature of that trauma. Conversion allows an individual to deal with psychological distress in some manner, in lieu of directly discussing the conflict or bringing it into conscious awareness.

Many examples of conversion signs are described in the clinical literature. Breuer and Freud presented the famous case of Anna O. in their *Studies on Hysteria* (1895). Anna O. was a young woman reportedly unable to use one arm, superficially resembling monoplegia. In the course of Breuer's work with the patient, she reported cradling her dying father in this arm. Breuer speculated her nonfunctional arm was symbolically representative of guilt about his death. Importantly, although not frequently reported in the psychoanalytic literature, Breuer described many other symptoms, including intermittent paraphasias, visual difficulties, deafness, headache, suicidal thoughts, anxiety, paresis/plegia, hallucinations, agitation, and absence-like spells (Breuer & Freud, 1895). Anna O. certainly met the initial (A) criterion for *DSM-IV* conversion disorder with "symptoms or deficits affecting voluntary motor or sensory function that suggest a neurological or other general medical condition" (American Psychiatric Association, 1994, p. 457). However, she also had numerous symptoms that would easily qualify her for a diagnosis of somatization by current *DSM* standards. In fact, it is rare to see a circumscribed neurological-appearing deficit in isolation. With minimal probing, the likelihood of unearthing a history of other neuropsychiatric symptoms and diagnoses is quite strong.

In clinical practice, the terms *conversion, somatization*, and *hysteria* are often used interchangeably. This fact suggests that clinical practitioners in a number of different areas of medicine and mental health continue to regard early psychodynamic notions of conversion as the essence of somatoform illness. The broadening of the conversion hysteria concept became the focus of Freud's work and developed into what we now know as classical psychoanalytic theory. Notably, unconscious conflicts are thought to underlie all manner of neuroses, whether they present as somatoform symptoms, depression, or anxiety. In practical terms, there is broad appeal in psychoanalytic notions about the development of psychopathology, including pathology expressed as somatization:

> Although there was disagreement among the early psychoanalytic psychosomaticists as to whether the symptoms of these diseases

have primary symbolic meaning, comparable to the symptoms of conversion hysteria, the different theoretical disease models they developed were all based on the notion that intrapsychic (especially preoedipal) conflicts, and the emotions associated with them, play a central role in the pathogenisis of disease. (Taylor et al., 1997, p. 217)

Psychoanalytically oriented notions can theoretically account for many psychological problems, but the extent to which they can do so is limited by a lack of falsifiability. Despite the dubious scientific status of psychoanalytic notions, they achieved considerable penetration in clinical reasoning, popular media, and public attitudes about psychopathology. The idea that early life experiences are crucial to ontology is now an unquestioned mental habit for both clinicians and laypersons. More scientifically minded theorists, however, attempted to merge psychoanalytic constructs with systematic observation and testable hypotheses. These endeavors led to the emergence of attachment theory (Bowlby, 1969).

Attachment and Early Developmental Theories of Somatization

Attachment theory focuses on the nature and quality of early infant relationships and how these affect subsequent emotional health and behavior. From the outset, Bowlby (1969) assumed that there were strong biologically mediated links in these relationships. Unlike the more abstract models of the early psychoanalysts, attachment theorists put forth a strong psychobiological model clearly suggesting that early experiences influence neural development, as well as subsequent behavior. This basic proposition has been more thoroughly developed by modern-day theorists (Schore, 1994, 2001, 2002). A good part of the appeal of the attachment model is its developmental focus, in contrast with the work of Freud, who studied primarily adults and adult psychopathology. Further, the other major influence on John Bowlby's early work, Charles Darwin, also developed his theories based on adults or mature species. As noted above, many theories about psychopathology and, more specifically, somatization tend to focus on biological factors or environmental/ psychological factors to the exclusion of the other side of the nature/nurture debate. The integrative nature of attachment theory, as well as its developmental perspective, is therefore a welcome synthesis of many important ideas developed over the past century or more. It also takes advantage of the wide knowledge base of those studying developmental phenomena and reminds us of the importance of understanding the dynamic nature of what it is we seek to describe in our typical clinical enterprise.

Bowlby (1969) and others were not specifically concerned with somatization, though their work has certainly had a significant influence on how we understand such clinical phenomena. As explained throughout this chapter, biological, behavioral, and psychodynamic theories have been used with varying degrees of success to explain somatoform symptoms. Because of Bowlby's (1969) reliance on traditional psychoanalytic theory, he and others certainly talked about hysteria (somatization) as resulting from problems with attachment, though this was not necessarily a major focus of that work. However, there has been a recent dramatic increase in studies seeking to examine the relationship between attachment, affect regulation, and somatoform disorders. The ability of the attachment model to incorporate biological and more traditional psychodynamic theories makes it attractive for researchers and clinicians. There are also a number of well-validated measures that allow researchers to quantify constructs that have emerged from attachment theory. As a result, numerous recent studies have examine the relationship between attachment styles and different symptom presentations (e.g., Ciechanowski, Walker, Katon, & Russo, 2002; Waldinger, Schulz, Barsky, & Ahern, 2006; Waller & Scheidt, 2006; Wearden, Cook, & Vaughan-Jones, 2003; Wearden, Lamberton, Crook, Walsh, 2005).

Before reviewing relevant studies, a few words about attachment theory are in order. Briefly, attachment theory states that all people develop "internal working models" based on their early experiences with important others. These cognitive (representational) models of self and others subsequently influence how an individual interacts with people, and the nature of their relationships (Bowlby, 1973). Ainsworth (1967) provided the earliest descriptions of different patterns of infant attachment, referring to four primary patterns: secure, anxious/avoidant, anxious/resistant, and disorganized/disoriented. These patterns were identified through the use of Ainsworth's "strange situation procedure," which became the standard for observing the interaction between infants and mothers/caregivers. Many different patterns have been proposed over the years, and it is beyond the scope of this discussion to review these, except as they relate to various studies examining the attachment construct with somatization patients.

Bartholomew and Horowitz (1991) presented a schema that identified two fundamental kinds of adult attachment: secure and insecure. Secure attachment is the result of an individual having a positive model of both self and

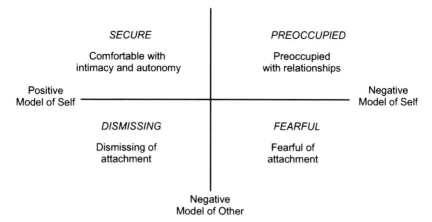

FIGURE 4.1. Bartholomew's four-category model of attachment.

others. Insecure attachments result from the other three possible combinations in a basic 2×2 matrix (see Figure 4.1): A positive model of self and a negative model of others results in a "dismissing" attachment style; a negative model of self and a positive model of others results in a "preoccupied" attachment style; and a negative model of self and a negative model of others results in a "fearful" attachment style.

Ciechanowski et al. (2002) examined a large group of female primary care HMO patients with respect to attachment style (Bartholomew & Horowitz, 1991), somatization symptoms, and health care utilization. They found that attachment style was significantly related to symptom reporting such that preoccupied and fearfully attached individuals showed a higher level of somatic symptom reporting compared to securely attached individuals. Ciechanowski et al. (2002) also noted a significant association between attachment style and primary care visits/costs. They found that patients with preoccupied attachment showed higher levels of utilization and primary care costs, while fearfully attached patients had the lowest utilization and costs. Interestingly, despite the fact that preoccupied and fearfully attached individuals both reported a high level of symptomatology, their utilization of services was quite different.

Schmidt, Strauss, and Braehler (2002) gave a sample of normal individuals a measure of attachment and a measure of subjective complaints. Their findings indicated that the highest level of physical symptomatology was seen in anxiously attached individuals, while individuals with secure attachment did not show a high level of specific symptom report.

Etiological Theories of Somatoform Disorders 41

Waller and Scheidt (2006) focused on the issue of affect regulation and how it relates to attachment theory. Dismissing attachment was related to defensive processing and restricted expression of emotions (alexithymia), and this pattern seemed to be strongly represented among those with somatoform disorders. In other words, individuals with high levels of somatoform symptomatology tended to have a positive view of themselves and a negative view of others. In the Ciechanowski et al. (2002) study described above, such patients were described as "compulsively self-reliant," and they did not show an increased pattern of somatic complaints or health care utilization relative to securely attached individuals.

A couple of recent studies examined childhood trauma more specifically as it relates to somatization symptoms, attachment style, and dissociation. Brown, Schrag, and Trimble (2005) sought to look at the occurrence of dissociation in somatizing patients as well as relating this to childhood interpersonal trauma and the nature of individuals' early family environments. While the study was not specifically interested in attachment, the focus on childhood trauma is consistent with an attachment model in general. Brown et al. (2005) failed to find a universal link between dissociative phenomena and somatization, noting that dissociation occurs in other medical populations to an equal extent. However, there was a general finding of chronic emotional abuse being strongly related to the development of somatization disorder. This seems consistent with what might generally be predicted within the attachment framework. The authors concluded that "many people with somatization disorder are exposed to an early environment that is emotionally cold, harsh, and characterized by frequent criticism, insults, rejection, and physical punishment" (p. 904).

Waldinger et al. (2006) also looked at the issue of childhood trauma, but within the framework of attachment theory. They looked at a community sample of 101 couples who completed a number of scales assessing relationships, childhood trauma, somatic symptoms, and general depressive symptomatology. Generally speaking, childhood trauma was related to higher levels of somatic symptom report and insecure attachment. Insecure attachment was independently related to higher levels of somatization, as well. In women, fearful attachment mediated the link between childhood trauma and somatization, while this relationship was not seen in men. Waldinger et al. (2006) concluded that in women childhood trauma is related to somatization because it brings about insecure adult attachment. In men, trauma and attachment are both predictors of somatization, but they do so independently. Regardless of differences based on gender, childhood trauma influences individuals' interpersonal relating skills.

Wearden et al. (2003) sought to determine whether there was an association between symptom reporting and coping with health problems and adult attachment style. They also looked at alexithymia as a mediating variable. Female undergraduates completed a number of questionnaires assessing attachment style, alexithymia, symptom reporting, and coping with health problems. Wearden et al. (2003) found a weak correlation between attachment, alexithymia, and negative affectivity. There was a strong association between alexithymia and insecure attachment. These researchers concluded that alexithymia develops as a result the interactions with caregivers, which also influences infant and adult attachment. The relationship between attachment and symptom reporting is hypothesized to be due to disturbances in regulating affect.

Finally, Wearden et al. (2005) sought to extend the findings from their earlier study using a four-category model of attachment as described in Bartholomew and Horowitz (1991). In this study, both male and female undergraduates completed questionnaire measures as described in Wearden et al. (2003). Findings from this study showed that fearful and preoccupied attachment styles were associated with increased symptom reporting, and that alexithymia has an additive effect on symptom reporting in fearfully attached individuals.

In general terms, a strong relationship has been noted between insecure attachment styles and reporting of physical symptoms. While many of the studies cited did not specifically examine these relationships in patients with somatoform symptoms or disorders, the fundamental relationship between (presumably) early relational trauma and subsequent problems with all manner of interpersonal communication, affect regulation, and attachment seems well established. Schore (1994, 2001, 2002) has written expansively on the topic of infant relational trauma and its effect on the development of the right hemisphere. He has integrated findings from the trauma literature and developmental psychopathology that point to the right hemisphere's dominance in early development. Far from simplistic notions about the right hemisphere being important in emotional processing, Schore (1994) and others have focused on the interrelationship between attachment, emotional processing, and the effects of trauma during critical periods in early development. Once again, the focus of much of this work has been on extremes of behavior and pathology. That is, dramatic clinical disorders such as posttraumatic stress disorder seem to draw the attention of researchers for a number of reasons. However, these models tend to emphasize the dynamic nature of early emotional experiences, maturation of neural circuitry, and the resulting effect on adaptive coping (Schore, 2002). The flexibility of such models allows for the common clinical observation of the fact that the same trauma results in markedly different clinical symptomatology from individual to individual. This would seem to be true whether we're talking about posttraumatic stress disorder or postconcussive syndrome. Of course, much work needs to be done to understand these relationships in clinical disorders that are more commonly seen by neuropsychologists. It seems likely that somatoform disorders, postconcussive syndrome, and all manner of disorders characterized by maladaptive coping likely fit somewhere on the spectrum of early relational trauma. Insights into these matters might well be obtained by examining attachment styles, alexithymia, and affect regulation as a more routine aspect of our clinical assessments.

Cultural Issues in Somatization

In the foregoing discussion, I have described various explanatory models or theories about somatization. In this section I present a brief discussion of cultural considerations, not as an explanatory model for understanding somatoform disorders, but rather as an acknowledgment of the importance of considering such factors in the clinical context. The nosological approach espoused in the *DSM* system emphasizes atheoretical description, which is frankly antithetical to appreciation of cultural factors in psychiatric diagnosis. In fact, many authors remark that the dualistic nature of the somatoform disorders category is particularly problematic for characterizing somatoform symptoms in individuals from non-Western cultures (González & Griffith, 1996; Kirmayer & Young, 1998; Kleinman, 1977; Mayou, Kirmayer, Simon, Kroenke, & Sharpe, 2005). While Western and European cultures have arguably made progress in destigmatizing mental illness, psychological explanations of various symptoms remain unpopular and unacceptable in many cultures.

The term *idioms of distress* (Nichter, 1981) is used frequently in the cross-cultural psychiatry and mental health literature. An idiom of distress allows otherwise pathological behaviors or experiences to be understood as a phenomenon of culture or social circumstances. The *DSM-IV* includes an appendix that provides descriptions of a number of such "culture-bound syndromes." This is presumably to assist the clinician in identifying culture-specific issues that might otherwise obscure appropriate diagnostic formulations. Kirmayer and Young (1998) proposed three broad idioms of distress that focus on themes of stress, pollution, and traumatic memories. The *stress idiom* is probably closest to widely held beliefs about the effects of stress on medical functioning in Western cultures. *Pollution* is more specific to the fact that many immigrants express concern about the lack of availability of certain foods or the difference in environments between their homeland and their current country of residence. The idiom of *traumatic memories* refers to the fact that many immigrants see the trauma of their former lives as well as the trauma of adjusting to sometimes dramatically different circumstances as causal factors in their general sense of unwellness. Of course, these notions are particularly important in understanding the experiences and symptoms of immigrants and how they react to sometimes very different cultural and climatic settings.

In a more general sense, Kirmayer et al. (2004) discuss difficulties with applying Western notions of somatoform disorders to various ethnic groups or cultures. A lack of understanding of culturally specific meanings of symptoms is often problematic. It is only through a more thorough understanding of a patient's social context that movement toward understanding the impact of stress and emotion on their physical symptoms is possible. Even so, the cost to an individual of taking a psychological view of their physical problems might have repercussions that are far more troubling than dealing with nagging physical symptoms. Kirmayer and Young (1998) also note a prevailing Western view that considers somatic symptoms as indicative of a more primitive or unsophisticated way of responding to psychological distress. Taking such a view, it is often the case that somatizing patients are considered poor candidates for psychotherapy. This is unfortunate, if only because it connotes a sense of therapeutic nihilism.

The neuropsychological literature on cross-cultural issues has generally been concerned with test development and the appropriateness of assessment approaches with various cultural subgroups (Poreh, 2002). Nonetheless, neuropsychologists are frequently asked to characterize patients' functional level and make recommendations regarding treatment possibilities. Thus, the neuropsychologist's responsibility is not a simple matter of assuring examiner language fluency (Artiola i Fortuny & Mullaney, 1998) or understanding the effects of illiteracy on assessment measures (Ardila, Roselli, & Puente, 1994), but rather a more wide-ranging appreciation of the patient's cultural background and motivation. Dana (1996) suggests that it is important to be able to characterize a patient's level of acculturation in order to provide appropriate evaluation and treatment services. He describes four outcome categories of acculturation: traditional, marginal, bicultural, and assimilated. *Traditional* individuals have essentially retained their original culture, whereas *assimilated* individuals have adopted the culture of the society in which they live. The extent to which an individual might benefit from mainstream treatments or with whom standard assessment measures can be validly employed is likely dictated by their level of acculturation—which in neuropsychological terms would mean language fluency, literacy, and a reasonable understanding of prevailing social standards. In neuropsychological assessment, the best-case scenario is that which allows the greatest dependence on chosen measures and standard normative databases. Presumably, the less assimilated a patient is, the greater the degree of "guesswork" needed in arriving at conclusions. Eventually, a point is reached where a valid assessment is not possible or advisable.

For the purposes of this discussion, one of the more interesting dilemmas faced by neuropsychologists is the assessment of immigrant patients in the context of personal injury or postconcussive syndrome claims. The use of symptom validity tests (SVTs) to assess effort, motivation, and possible malingering is a widely accepted and recommended practice (Larrabee, 2005a; Sweet, 1999). The ability to make diagnostic distinctions between somatoform disorders, factitious disorders, and malingering often hinges on patients' performances on these measures. Nonetheless, there are no published studies evaluating the use of SVTs with immigrant populations. My own experience with measures such as the Test of Memory Malingering (Tombaugh, 1996) and the Word Memory Test (Green, Allen, & Astner, 1996) with immigrant individuals is that there is a very high failure rate compared to recommended cut-off scores. Poreh (2002) surmises that patients failing these measures are likely characterized by "traditional" or "marginal" levels of acculturation (Dana, 1996). It might indeed be the case that their difficulties represent a modified idiom of distress or an extension of a similar problem from their past.

In summary, consideration of cultural issues is very important when working with patients from diverse backgrounds. The meaning of certain symptom presentations can be very different in different cultures, and this can affect the accuracy and relevance of assessment data and subsequent treatment recommendations. The interface between somatoform syndromes in neuropsychological practice with immigrant populations likely represents a very small portion of most practices. Nevertheless, the situations need to be managed with sensitivity and understanding.

5

Somatoform Disorders and Neuropsychological Assessment

Neuropsychological Symptoms and Somatization

Cognitive Dysfunction in Somatization, Medical Patients,
and Normal Samples

The nature of somatoform disorders is such that studies of specific neuro-cognitive deficits within these disorders are rare. Indeed, studying memory or executive dysfunction in a disorder with equivocal or no specific neuropathology would be an unusual tack to take. Rather, more general examination of neuropsychological abilities has typically been the preferred approach when describing the cognitive concomitants of somatoform disorders. Binder (2005) notes the nonspecific nature of general symptoms in somatoform disorders and emphasizes the fact that cognitive complaints are typically not specific to a diagnosis. Such symptom reports also tend to be more strongly associated with neuropsychiatric distress than they are with actual pathology or identified cognitive deficits (Binder, Kindermann, Heaton, & Salinsky et al., 1998; Landre, Poppe, Davis, Schmaus, & Hobbs, 2006; Larrabee & Levin, 1986; Wilson, Arnold, Schneider, Li, & Bennett, 2007).

The relationship between reported cognitive difficulties and somatoform symptoms, particularly those involving emotional distress, is not specific to somatoform disorders and is reported in a wide range of neurological and medical conditions. Many studies flesh out this relationship and are helpful for providing a broader conceptual framework for how we look at somatizing patients (Brands et al., 2006, 2007; Castellon et al., 2004; Wilson et al., 2007). Some recent examples of studies are reviewed here to illustrate the fact that medically unexplained symptoms are not solely in the domain of somatoform disorders or functional somatic syndromes. Further, complaints about cognitive difficulties are rather common and are most often associated with distress in a generic sense.

For instance, a couple of recent studies by Brands and colleagues have shown that patients with both type 1 (Brands et al., 2006) and type 2 diabetes (Brands et al., 2007) report higher levels of neuropsychiatric symptomatology than do controls. Type 2 diabetic patients show greater neuropathology on MRI studies, greater psychological distress, and greater cognitive impairment than do matched controls. However, no relationship was noted between objective cognitive impairment and neuropsychiatric symptomatology (Brands et al., 2007). In type 1 diabetic patients, there were few neuropathological findings and less overall distress than seen in older, type 2 patients or in controls, suggesting little neuropathology in hyperglycemic patients. However, patients continued to show more neuropsychiatric symptomatology and more reported cognitive difficulty (compared to controls) despite a continued lack of association with actual deficits on neuropsychological measures (Brands et al., 2006).

In disorders where there is a combination of neuropathology, risk factors, and cognitive dysfunction (and strong associations between these factors), neuropsychiatric distress tends to be reported at high levels. Distress is consistently related to complaints about cognitive functioning, rather than objective imaging or cognitive findings. For instance, Castellon et al. (2004) studied a group of breast cancer survivors regarding cognitive problems that have been reported related to adjuvant chemotherapy. Their findings focused on the ill effects of chemotherapy on cognitive functioning but once again showed a lack of association between complaints of cognitive functioning and actual neuropsychological test performance.

Wilson et al. (2007) described a strong association between chronic distress and dementia in late life, though distress was not related to typical neuropathological findings or to specific cognitive deficits. This led these researchers to conclude that perhaps stress has a neurodegenerative effect, but one that is independent of typically cited pathological findings in dementia. Such a proposal is compatible with etiological aspects of somatoform disorders discussed in chapter 4 and suggests the possibility of some manner of cerebral dysfunction, though not necessarily a kind that would be identified with typical neuropsychological assessment measures. Of course, this notion undergirds current neuropsychiatric notions about affective and mental disorders in general.

Thus, the relationship between reported cognitive difficulties and neuro-psychiatric distress is well known, as is the lack of relationship between the report of cognitive difficulties and actual performance on standard measures. It is beyond the scope of this discussion to review the numerous studies showing this relationship, except to note that it exists in a range of conditions, from normal individuals to those with medical illness and no clear neurological involvement, to those with clear underlying neurological disease (Cull et al, 1996; Grace, Nielson, Hopkins, & Berg, 1999; Hinkin et al., 1996; Rourke, Halman, & Bassel, 1999; Vermeulen, Aldenkamp, & Alpherts, 1993; Wang, Chan, & Deng, 2006). In this general context, memory difficulties and other vague neuropsychological complaints might serve as a sort of cognitive idiom of distress. People who feel unwell—for all manner of reasons—also tend to feel like their cognitive functioning is poor. At least as far as standard neuropsychological measures are concerned, this relationship is difficult to establish. It is not unreasonable to assume that the measures we employ clinically are simply not sensitive enough to pick up on relatively subtle difficulties, particularly in populations that might be described as having subclinical neurological risk factors. Alternatively, it is not unreasonable to assume that no "real" cognitive difficulties exist. This latter view seems to hold considerable sway in modern-day neuropsychology practice, particularly in the forensic realm.

Beyond the legions of unwell-feeling individuals, there is an important literature on the base rates of cognitive complaints in normal or "well" individuals. Several studies examining base rates of reported cognitive difficulties provide important glimpses into the nature of complaints in normal individuals (Fox, Lees-Haley, Earnest, & Dolezal-Wood, 1995; Gouvier, Cubic, Jones, Brantley, & Cutlip, 1992; Gouvier, Uddo-Crane, & Brown, 1988; Hilsabeck, Gouvier, & Bolter, 1998; Martin, Hayes, & Gouvier, 1996; Roberts, Varney, Hulbert, & Paulsen, 1990). These studies typically show that certain symptoms thought to be characteristic of postconcussive syndrome (PCS) are fairly common in normal individuals, or that symptoms reported by patients are not far outside the range of normative expectation. The distributions of normal and clinical samples are likely overlapping with respect to complaints about cognitive dysfunction. Thus, in both clinical and normal samples, there is a range of symptom acknowledgment, and normalcy is clearly not an either/or distinction.

The relationship that we understand most clearly is that between psychological distress and the report of symptoms. Reporting cognitive dysfunction may be more a way of communicating distress and discomfort than of indicating problems within a specific domain of cognitive functioning. It is often the case that patients' reports do not correspond to deficits as conceptualized and evaluated by neuropsychologists. That is, "memory problems" might actually be problems with word finding, attention, or new learning, or they might simply reflect a patient's anxiety or malaise. In clinical neuropsychology, this underscores the importance of a thorough psychological evaluation.

Psychological Disturbance in Somatization

The cognitive correlates of somatization are difficult to characterize conceptually. In contrast, psychological correlates of somatization are well known and well captured by clinical instruments that are routinely employed in the neuropsychological evaluation. The Minnesota Multiphasic Personality Inventory–2 (MMPI-2; Butcher, Dahlstrom, Graham, Tellegen, & Kaemmer, 1989) is the most widely employed personality and psychopathology measure in the world (Graham, 2006), and its ability to identify individuals with somatoform features is well established. Scale 3, Hysteria (Hy), is described by Graham (2006) as having been developed to "identify patients who were having hysterical reactions to stress situations." Dated terminology notwithstanding, the scale has long been effective in identifying individuals who report high levels of specific somatic symptoms, including such items as chest pain, nausea, and headaches. Other items involve denial of psychological or emotional problems, and naiveté/optimism with regard to how they view others. The 60 items composing Hy in the MMPI-2 were all carried over from the original MMPI (Hathaway & McKinley, 1943). Thus, the original conception of hysteria used to develop the original MMPI Hy scale seems to have held up quite well, psychometrically speaking, over the years.

Scale 1, Hypochondriasis, was originally developed to assess a sense of preoccupation with the body and disease states, though high scorers on this scale often tend to be characterized as having somatoform disorders (Graham, 2006). However, it is the combination of elevated scores on scales 1 and 3, with a considerably lower score on scale 2, Depression (D), that is most clearly characteristic of individuals with somatization and somatoform disorders. Descriptions of the so-called "conversion V" profile typically focus on the fact that individuals with this profile tend to present themselves as normal and strongly resistant to psychological interpretations of their discomfort. They are generally seen as immature and needy and are dependent on others for emotional support. Patients with the conversion V are often resentful and hostile, though unlikely to act out. It has long been thought that their prognosis in psychotherapy is poor because of a lack of insight (Graham, 2006). Fortunately, recent work that has been more integrative, including cognitive behavior therapy techniques and the fostering of emotional awareness, has been successful in working with these individuals (Woolfolk & Allen, 2007).

The interpretive terms "faking" and "malingering" have connotations that are contentious and inflammatory. Irrespective of the validity of the label in a particular somatizing patient/claimant, negative clinical and medicolegal consequences accompany such diagnoses. It is primarily in forensic contexts that such terms are encountered, because the purpose of most civil proceedings is to distinguish genuine from trivial damages. That is not the case in purely clinical settings (although somatizing claimants may use clinical opportunities toward civil ends). In this context, neuropsychologists are often asked to rule out malingering or the purposeful production of false symptoms in order to secure some kind of "secondary gain." Secondary gain is defined as an external incentive to prolong symptom reporting beyond reasonable recovery times. Examples include compensation, attendant care services for family members unable to find better paying work, access to narcotic medications, and societal forgiveness of the adult expectation to work. Cases often rest on the validity of assessment data. Therefore, determinations about the validity of symptom reports and cognitive dysfunction are central to these proceedings. While these issues are certainly important in the forensic context, the use of such terms in the clinical setting is probably more confrontational than is reasonable or useful. There is an implicit assumption that a high level of unusual symptom reporting, particularly in the physical realm, is compatible with a diagnosis of malingering, or at least exaggeration. Larrabee (2005b, p. 117) notes that there are three patterns of malingering often seen in the neuropsychological context: "false or exaggerating reporting of symptoms," "intentionally poor performance on neuropsychological tests," or "a combination of symptom exaggeration and intentional performance deficit." The first of these patterns obviously has significant overlap with what is expected and reported in various somatoform disorders.

Neuropsychologists have been at the forefront of developing scales to assess the nature of complaints or symptoms reported on the MMPI-2. The Lees-Haley Fake Bad Scale (FBS; Lees-Haley, English, & Glenn, 1991) has emerged as a reliable and valid indicator of somatic symptom exaggeration, with most of the research on this measure emanating from the forensic arena (e.g., Larrabee, 2005b; Lees-Haley, Iverson, Lange, Fox, & Allen, 2002; Nelson,

Sweet, & Demakis, 2006). Among the numerous validity indices available for use with the MMPI-2, the FBS has been shown to be particularly effective in forensic contexts. The FBS consists of 43 items, which were selected to be sensitive to exaggeration of personal injury (Lees-Haley, 1992; Lees-Haley et al., 1991), though there has been some debate about its effectiveness in doing so (Arbisi & Butcher, 2004; Butcher, Arbisi, Atlis, & McNulty, 2003). Nonetheless, the publishers of the MMPI-2 have recently acknowledged the measure's empirical basis and effectiveness as a validity indicator. Ben-Porath and Tellegen (2006) state that "empirical research has established the utility of the scale in identifying potentially exaggerated claims of disability, primarily in the context of forensic neuropsychological evaluations." They further note that

> scores above 22 should raise concerns about the validity of self-reported symptoms and that raw scores above 28 should raise very significant concerns about the validity of self-reported symptoms, particularly with individuals for whom relevant physical injury or medical problems have been ruled out.

Numerous recent studies have begun to flesh out the psychometric properties of the FBS as well as provide data on the accuracy of clinical and forensic decision making based on this and other validity indicators (Greiffenstein, Baker, Gola, Donders, & Miller; Larrabee, 2005b; Martens, Donders, & Millis, 2001; Nelson et al., 2006).

The major distinction between the clinical and forensic contexts concerns identifiable external incentives or secondary gain. The *DSM-IV* description of factitious disorders allows that patients can willfully distort or misrepresent their symptoms, though the motivation is to assume a sick role rather than collect some kind of incentive such as money or the avoidance of work or legal entanglements. As mentioned in chapter 4, distinctions regarding the willfulness of behavior and presumed "reinforcers" are difficult to make with certainty. In the forensic context, however, there is typically a clear and concrete secondary gain issue. In the absence of such clear external incentives, the goal of psychological and neuropsychological assessment becomes more related to understanding and changing behavior. Therefore, while measures such as FBS are impressive in their ability to identify exaggeration, it is important to be mindful of the context of an assessment and to interpret results of specific indices accordingly. Butcher and colleagues (Arbisi & Butcher, 2004; Butcher et al., 2003) appeared to be making this clinical argument by suggesting that the FBS might overdiagnose malingering in clinical settings where there were no forensic issues or in psychiatric samples. In making this argument, they assailed the psychometric properties of the FBS, though not in a very convincing manner. Numerous subsequent studies have indicated that the psychometric properties of FBS are quite sound and equal to or better than traditional MMPI-2 validity measures (e.g., Greiffenstein, Baker, Axelrod, Peck, & Gervais, 2004; Greiffenstein, Fox, & Lees-Haley, 2007; Nelson et al., 2006).

In the context of a forensic evaluation, an elevated FBS score might well suggest a greater likelihood of exaggeration and/or malingering. Without such a context, what is behind a high level of somatic symptom reporting is less clear. That is, a patient's acknowledgment of significant somatoform symptoms does not, de facto, suggest that the patient is necessarily doing so for some kind of secondary gain. Clearly, the use of such negatively charged labels can be alienating for patients. This is not to say that symptom exaggeration does not occur and that it should not be labeled as such, though the use of pejorative labels such as "faking" and "malingering" run the risk of prejudicing future providers and might limit treatment potential. In summary, the FBS scale might reasonably be thought of as an indication of "somatic distress" not unlike the "F" scale as a more general indicator of distress or "demoralization."

A recent study by Henry, Heilbronner, Mittenberg, & Enders (2006) described an empirically derived MMPI-2 subscale (the Henry–Heilbronner Index, or HHI) that was developed to assess symptom exaggeration in personal injury and disability claims. These authors suggest that the HHI was superior to the FBS and other validity scales with regard to identifying exaggeration, overreporting, or malingering of physical symptoms on the MMPI-2. They suggest that it is a "pseudosomatic index" that should perform as well or better than such measures as FBS and MMPI-2 clinical scales 1 and 3. Again, it is important to note that many of the scales from the forensic context are particularly useful in identifying exaggeration in individuals who are being assessed for the purpose of disability determination or generally in the medicolegal context.

The Response Bias Scale (RBS; Gervais, 2005; Gervais, Ben-Porath, Wygant, & Green, in press) was developed from work based on MMPI-2 responses from disability claimants who failed Green's Word Memory Test (WMT; Green, 2003). Specifically, the RBS consists of 39 items that discriminated between non-head-injured disability claimants who passed and failed the WMT. Nelson, Sweet, and Heilbronner (2007) compared the RBS and other MMPI-2 validity scales with respect to their ability to distinguish between patients with secondary gain or no secondary gain issues. These authors found that the RBS correlated significantly with the FBS and most traditional validity scales in both groups of patients. The RBS had the largest between-group effect size, with FBS running a close second. Nelson et al. (2007) concluded that the RBS appears to be similar to the FBS in terms of measuring symptom validity in the forensic context.

Other personality and symptom measures have been examined in the neuropsychological context, though certainly not to the extent of the MMPI-2 and its numerous validity indices. For example, the Personality Assessment Inventory (PAI; Morey, 1991) appears to be increasingly popular in clinical settings. Wagner, Wymer, Topping, and Pritchard (2005) described an "NES indicator," which is a score calculated from the PAI somatization subscales. This index was found to distinguish between patients with nonepileptic seizures (NESs) and epileptic seizures (ESs) with reasonably good sensitivity and specificity. In contrast, Sumanti, Boone, Savodnik, and Gorsuch (2006) failed to detect any relationship between PAI validity indices and standard neuropsychological measures of effort in a sample of workers' compensation "stress" claimants. It is likely that additional studies assessing the utility of various somatization and validity indicators from the PAI will emerge as more sizable databases emerge.

Larrabee (2007) reviews a number of measures that have been examined specifically in terms of the development of malingering indices, including the Revised Symptom Checklist 90 (Derogatis, 1992) and the Illness Behavior Questionnaire (Pilowsky & Spence, 1983). These measures have been more typically used in evaluating pain patients with injury claims. There is little in the neuropsychological literature examining these inventories in somatizing patients, regardless of litigation status. Screening measures such as the Beck Depression Inventory attempt to sample specific elements of neuropsychiatric disorders, though they tend to be broadly associated with distress. Obviously, the relationship between somatoform symptomatology and general distress is strongly positive. However, as mentioned above, these kinds of measures tend to show little relationship with actual cognitive impairment. Rather, they provide a very basic sense of the somatoform patient's distress, which we know is most strongly related to reported symptoms, not actual deficits. Woolfolk and Allen (2007) mention a number of specific measures of somatization and somatoform symptomatology that have been used in treatment studies with somatizing patients. These are not typical measures that are employed in clinical settings, unless the specific goal or function is to treat somatoform disorders in a structured and very standardized fashion—in other words, not the context in which most neuropsychologists practice.

Disorders/Syndromes Associated With Somatization

Binder and Campbell (2004) describe a wide range of conditions, including pseudoneurological illness, silicone breast implant illness, fibromyalgia, chronic fatigue syndrome (CFS), multiple chemical sensitivities (MCS), toxic mold and sick building syndrome, and Persian Gulf War–related illnesses. They used the term *somatic stress disorders* to "represent the actual manifestation of physical symptoms due at least partially in response to physically experienced or psychologically perceived stressors." The list was by no means exhaustive, but rather reflected the somatoform "flavors of the month" likely to be encountered in neuropsychological assessment practices. To the extent that these disorders have been systematically examined with neuropsychological measures, it has typically been the case that "impairment" has been noted—a trend that dates back to work done by early leaders in the field of clinical neuropsychology (Matthews, Shaw, & Klove, 1966).

Binder's reviews on medically unexplained symptoms (Binder, 2005; Binder & Campbell, 2004) are comprehensive and provide both a chronological sense of the nature of studies conducted, and a syndromal view of how different somatoform disorders have been studied. It would seem to follow that different syndromes would be expected to present with more or less neuropsychological impairment as a function of proposed mechanisms of dysfunction, or at least the beliefs about such mechanisms on the part of those afflicted. For instance, a pseudoneurological disorder such as NESs would seem more likely to present with cognitive deficits than would fibromyalgia, and still more likely than irritable bowel syndrome. Based on the current literature, it would appear that work done in the past has had the general effect of answering questions about the existence of cognitive impairment and/or neuropathology in various somatoform disorders. In the future, fewer studies on neuropsychological impairment in fibromyalgia seem likely, while studies examining such deficits in mild traumatic brain injury (mTBI) will continue until such a time as these relationships are determined to be clearly established. In this context, the import and value of numerous symptom validity measures cannot be overstated. Within neuropsychological practice, such measures have shifted the focus from identifying ethereal cognitive deficits to characterizing the psychological and developmental aspects of patients with such presentations. Nevertheless, a review of these syndromes and the studies conducted is worthwhile to place current work in the appropriate context. I briefly review literature examining neuropsychological functioning in syndromes ranging from those that are not likely neurologically based (e.g., fibromyalgia) to those that might well invoke an underlying neurological basis. In the latter group, I include some disorders and diseases whose etiologies continue to be hotly debated (e.g., mTBI/PCS), as well as some with clear underlying neuropathology (e.g., multiple sclerosis [MS]).

Fibromyalgia, Chronic Fatigue, and Chronic Pain

Fibromyalgia, CFS, and chronic pain presentations have long been linked in terms of the number of symptoms they share and a lack of definitive diagnostic markers. These presentations and syndromes involve fatigue, sleep disturbance, memory and concentration complaints, and neuropsychiatric features, including depression and anxiety symptoms. There has been no shortage of earnest attempts to understand the nature of cognitive difficulties reported in these disorders, though clear relationships between reported cognitive deficits and purported disease mechanisms are lacking (Busichio, Tiersky, DeLuca, & Natelson, 2004; Cote & Moldofsky, 1997; DeLuca, Johnson, & Natelson, 1993; Glass, Park, Minear, & Crofford, 2005; Grace et al., 1999; Hart, Martelli, & Zasler, 2000; Iverson and McCracken, 1997; Landro, Stiles, & Sletvold, 1997; Munoz & Esteve, 2005; Park, Glass, Minear, & Crofford, 2001; Suhr, 2003; Tiersky, Johnson, Lange, Natelson, & DeLuca, 1997). Most studies in this area have reported performance deficits on a range of neuropsychological measures involving basic attention/concentration, information processing speed, motor speed and agility, and working memory. What is less clear is the relationship among objective cognitive deficits, subjective cognitive complaints, and neuropsychiatric distress. Methodologies employed in these various studies vary significantly, and it is difficult to arrive at firm conclusions due to differences in how patient samples are identified, the nature of cognitive measures employed, the definition of cognitive impairment, and the ability to account for confounding factors in performance.

Suhr (2003) reported a study that accounted for a number of these different variables. She compared fibromyalgia patients with chronic pain and healthy comparison groups to allow clear distinctions to be drawn with respect to important subject characteristics. Several psychological measures of relevance were included assessing subjective cognitive complaints, depressive symptomatology, and levels of fatigue. Neuropsychological domains were evaluated with widely used measures of general intellectual functioning, visual and verbal memory, attention/working memory, complex psychomotor speed, and, importantly, an embedded measure of effort. Unlike several of the studies listed above, Suhr (2003) did not find significant differences between clinical groups on the neuropsychological measures, nor was there significant impairment (i.e., two or more standard deviations below accepted clinical norms). General difficulties on cognitive tests were strongly associated with reported level of depression, pain, and fatigue, though this was true for all subject groups. This finding is consistent with what is reported in studies across a range of somatoform disorders and general medical conditions, as discussed above. Suhr (2003) provides a good example of how validity measures can facilitate more realistic research designs to assure that the results reflect the actual clinical state of affairs, and allow the opportunity to select out individuals that are clearly not putting forth adequate effort.

Busichio et al. (2004) acknowledged that they included the Test of Memory Malingering (TOMM; Tombaugh, 1996) as an effort measure in their CFS group, though only 34 of their final sample of 141 patients received the measure, because it was added to the protocol at a later date. This group has clearly been the most active in terms of neuropsychological studies in CFS (e.g., Busichio et al., 2004; DeLuca et al., 1993; Tiersky et al., 1997), so it is both encouraging and somewhat troubling to note this trend so late in the development of their research program.

While there has clearly been interest in studies on CFS and fibromyalgia, much of the work published in the 1990s and the early part of this decade has frankly been methodologically weak. More recently, studies examining symptom validity measures with patients presenting with fibromyalgia, chronic pain, and other such disorders have consistently found an overrepresentation of invalid responding or, at the very least, suspect effort (Bianchini, Greve, & Glynn, 2005; Gervais, Green, Allen, & Iverson, 2002; Rohling, Green, Allen, & Iverson, 2002). It has become increasingly clear that effort and motivation are major contributors to the variance in samples applying for disability, and a substantial number of patients with CFS, fibromyalgia, and chronic pain are disabled or seeking disability status (Arnow et al., 2006; Wolfe, Ross, Anderson, Russell, & Hebert, 1995).

Multiple Chemical Sensitivities/Idiopathic Environmental Intolerances

The neuropsychological literature on MCS or what is now referred to as idiopathic environmental intolerances (IEI) has been much less extensive than that in fibromyalgia, CFS, and chronic pain. Much of this literature consists of polemics and debates about the existence, or lack thereof, of a syndrome that sounds very much like what was described in the preceding section: patients reporting a range of vague symptoms, including confusion, fatigue, dizziness, nausea, and respiratory problems. The difference is that in MCS, the symptoms are typically preceded by exposure to any of a wide range of chemicals or substances found in the environment. The substances are typically irritants rather than known neurotoxins.

Labarge and McCaffrey (2000) reviewed what little research there was on the neuropsychological concomitants of MCS. Two studies by Fiedler and colleagues (Fiedler, Kipen, DeLuca, & Kelly-McNeil, 1996; Fiedler, Kipen, Deluca, Kelly-McNeil, & Natelson, 1994) compared patients with MCS to normal individuals and patients with CFS. No patients in these studies were involved in litigation, and there was essentially no relationship between the MCS designation and cognitive impairment. Similar findings were reported by Simon, Daniell, Stockbridge, Claypoole, & Rosenstock (1993), who compared MCS patients to those with chronic musculoskeletal injuries. While there were some difficulties with immediate recall of prose in the MCS group, any minor differences between the groups was eliminated when depression and anxiety symptoms were statistically controlled. A more recent study (Österberg, Orbæk, & Karlson, 2002) examined performance of MCS patients on several neuropsychological measures with demographically matched controls. The MCS group showed slower complex reaction time, which was not eliminated by correction for mental distress. Nonetheless, all other scores were within normal limits and not different from the comparison sample.

Labarge and McCaffrey (2000) noted that MCS individuals are often involved in litigation and that none of the studies they cited used any standardized measures of symptom validity. As noted above, the consistent lack of compelling neuropsychological test data in studies of medically unexplained symptoms will cause research studies to evolve and focus on the psychological profiles of individuals with such clinical presentations.

Along those lines, a couple of very recent studies have examined the nature of complaints in MCS/IEI patients with the MMPI-2 FBS scale. Binder, Storzbach, and Salinsky (2006) compared MMPI-2 profiles of patients with MCS, ESs, and NESs. All of the MCS patients were in litigation and showed significantly higher scores on FBS and MMPI-2 scales 1, 2, and 3 than either of the seizure groups. Staudenmayer and Phillips (2007) also examined MMPI-2 profiles, including the FBS, in a sample of litigating patients with IEI. Traditional validity scales (F, F$_B$, F$_P$, F-K) did not suggest overreporting of psychopathology, though half of the cases showed elevations on L and K scales. The authors report that one-fourth to one-half of individuals in this sample showed elevations on the FBS (depending upon various cut-offs), suggesting overreporting of unauthenticated symptoms. This contrasts with the findings of Binder et al. (2006), who reported significant elevations in 11 of 14 MCS cases. The clinical scale profiles were fairly typical somatization profiles, including elevations on scales 1 and 3 for females and scales 1, 2, and 3 for males. Staudenmayer and Phillips (2007) suggest that these patients see themselves as

> virtuous people without psychological or behavioral difficulties beyond those subsequent to environmental exposure. Their bias is to express stress and distress through somatization by emphasizing physical symptoms and denying psychological symptoms. (p. 67)

Such a portrayal describes many with somatoform disorders.

Overall, patients with MCS/IEI tend to show less in the way of significant cognitive impairment compared to other somatoform disorders, and their MMPI-2 clinical scales show a fairly characteristic conversion V. Two recent studies suggest that there are some differences in scores on the FBS in litigating samples, with Binder et al. (2006) reporting a very high level of FBS elevation and Staudenmayer and Phillips (2007) reporting relatively less significant elevation.

Nonepileptic Seizures

As noted in chapter 1, neurological or "nervous" symptoms have been a focus of clinical interest for hundreds of years. More specifically, "fits" or "spells" provide an interesting window into the inner workings of somatizing patients. Unlike patients with fibromyalgia, CFS, and chronic pain, NES patients produce a much more specific set of behaviors and symptoms. NESs can manifest in a number of ways, though the seizure or event itself provides important clinical information about the person experiencing the event. While NES patients often present with a range of somatoform symptoms, the focus of their disorder is the seizure. Neurologists specializing in diagnosis and treatment of seizure disorders are called *epileptologists*, and they are often associated with centers and programs that focus solely on patients with seizure-related problems. Thus, there tends to be less ambiguity in the diagnostic process for individuals who present clinically with seizures. There are standard protocols for making a determination about the nature of the patient's seizure behavior, which typically involves video-EEG monitoring, neuroimaging studies, and psychological/neuropsychological assessment. As such, the ability to rule out primary neurological disease or medical illness is much greater than is typical of such disorders as CFS, fibromyalgia, or MCS/IEI.

A number of neuropsychological studies have included NES patients as a group of primary interest or as a comparison sample with documented ES patients (Binder, Kindermann, Heaton, & Salinsky, 1998; Brown, Levin, Ramsay, & Katz, 1991; Drane et al., 2006; Locke, Berry, Fakhoury, & Schmitt, 2006; Matthews et al., 1966; Wilkus, Dodrill, & Thompson, 1984). The majority of these studies have found that patients with NES tend to be impaired to a similar degree as those with ES. That is, both ES and NES groups have shown impairment relative to normal control samples. For instance, in one of the earliest studies known to make such a comparison, Wilkus et al. (1984) found that roughly half of both ES and NES groups produced abnormal scores on a standard test battery. Brown et al. (1991) found no differences between ES and NES groups on several neuropsychological measures, though NES patients were inconsistent relative to patients with ESs. A more recent study by Locke et al. (2006) also failed to identify group differences between NES and ES patients, though they proposed different mechanisms for the impairment observed in the respective groups.

Binder, Salinsky, and Smith (1994) compared groups that were diagnosed with ES and "psychogenic seizures" via EEG monitoring. They compared patients on a number of measures, including the Portland Digit Recognition Test (PDRT), the MMPI-2, and some bedside cognitive measures. The results indicated that NES patients performed more poorly on the PDRT and that this was associated with somatoform MMPI profiles, and made more errors on the basic screening tests. The authors suggested that the PDRT performance of psychogenic seizure patients, while not comparable to that of malingerers, was inconsistent with respect to effort (Binder et al., 1994).

The preceding section described Binder et al.'s (2006) comparison of patients with NES, MCS, and ESs. In this small sample, MCS patients showed consistently higher FBS scores compared to regression-based estimates of FBS from ES and NES patients. Raw MMPI-2 data were not available because the seizure groups were selected from a previously published study (Binder et al., 1994). Eight of 14 NES patients in this report were seeking disability, while none of the ES patients was. Further, three of five NES patients who were given the PDRT failed the measure, suggesting inadequate effort, at the very least.

The MCS group was characterized by 5 of 14 individuals failing at least one neuropsychological symptom validity measure, which is actually a lower percentage of failure compared to available symptom validity data for the selected NES group. In other words, there is uncertainty about the direct comparability of these samples. Despite the unknowns, the NES sample was essentially intermediate to the MCS and ES samples with respect to the MMPI-2 profiles. They showed a traditional conversion V profile in the aggregate, as well as an elevated scale 8 (schizophrenia), which is likely due to the neurological nature of their complaints, including pervasive concerns about problems with thinking or "losing one's mind." Sorting through issues of motivation, litigation, and the nature of performance is becoming the focus of research with somatoform disorders.

A recent study by Drane et al. (2006) is a good example of how important it is to account for these variables. Not unlike the Suhr (2003) study examining fibromyalgia patients, this study examined groups of ES and NES patients on a number of neuropsychological measures. Drane et al. (2006) also included a standardized symptom validity measure, the WMT (Green, 2003). These authors noted that most previous studies did not account for the fact that a high percentage of patients with somatoform disorders tend to perform in a manner that suggests variable or inadequate effort. In fact, Drane et al. (2006) found that more than 50% of their NES sample failed the WMT (similar to the limited available data in Binder et al., 2006), compared to only 8% of the ES group. Further, NES patients who passed the WMT showed less objective impairment as measured by neuropsychological testing, MRI imaging, and video-EEG monitoring.

Cragar, Berry, Fakhoury, Cibula, and Schmitt (2006) specifically examined performance of patients in an epilepsy monitoring unit with respect to performance on a number of symptom validity measures. The authors compared performance of ES, NES, and combined (both ES and NES) groups on four measures of symptom validity. Their results suggested that 22% of patients with ES and 24% of patients with NES failed one or more of these effort measures. Interestingly, only 11% of the patients with both ES and NES performed below traditional cut-offs. These percentages are considerably less than those reported by Drane et al. (2006), and they also indicate a high level of failure on symptom validity measures in a clear neurological sample (ES). Certainly, the nature of the measures used and a seemingly more selected sample might account for some of the differences noted in the Cragar et al. (2006) and Drane et al. (2006) studies. Nonetheless, significant differences are emerging with regard to a different clinical samples perform on measures of symptom validity and effort. Much work is yet to be done to establish relationships among these variables.

Preliminary studies with clinical (particularly nonlitigating) samples of somatizing patients are intriguing and seem to call into question findings from the many studies that did not assess effort or motivation. It is clear that future studies will need to account for these factors. More important, finding such as those noted by Suhr (2003) and Drane et al. (2006) align neuropsychological test findings with imaging and electrographic findings suggesting no neurological impairment in these group of patients and helps to refocus the nature of inquiry going forward.

Postconcussive Syndrome Following Mild Traumatic Brain Injury
Definitions and disagreements about PCS following mTBI continue to litter the clinical neuropsychology landscape, and it is certainly well beyond the scope of this chapter to delve into those contentious issues to any degree. However, in the spirit of the preceding sections in this chapter, it has become increasingly clear that PCS following mTBI is a clinical entity moderated by a number of factors, including premorbid psychological functioning, litigation status, and motivation/effort (Binder, Rohling, & Larrabee, 1997; Dikmen, Machamer, Winn, & Temkin, 1995; Frencham, Fox, & Maybery, 2005; Greiffenstein & Baker, 2006; Iverson & Binder, 2000; Larrabee, 2005c; McAllister, 2005; Ross, Millis, Krukowski, Putnam, & Adams, 2004; Suhr, Tranel, Wefel, & Barrash, 1997). In this sense, PCS is much like many other somatic distress disorders. In addition to cognitive deficits of a legitimate sort (Binder et al., 1997; Dikmen et al., 1995; Frencham et al., 2005), patients with PCS are often plagued by a range of vague symptoms, such as fatigue, confusion, dizziness, pain, and emotional distress. In the case of head injury, such symptoms are frequently inversely related to the severity of injury (e.g., Dikmen et al., 1995; Greiffenstein & Baker, 2006).

Several studies and reviews have clarified the nature of cognitive deficits following mTBI (Binder et al., 1997; Dikmen et al., 1995; Frencham et al., 2005; Schretlen & Shapiro, 2003), though many earlier studies did not benefit from the use of symptom validity measures to assure the validity of data collected. The sports concussion literature has provided considerable and compelling data indicating that neuropsychological recovery from concussion in athletes is typically complete within one week to one month of the trauma (Collins et al., 1999; McCrea et al., 2003). The importance of this line of work in the broader clinical context was to suggest that individuals who are healthy and well motivated typically recover from concussion or mTBI quickly and fully. Of course, health and motivation in our typical clinical samples can be extremely variable, and it seems unwise to make assumptions about these factors when conducting good clinical research.

As mentioned above, it is not my goal to provide a comprehensive review of the mTBI or concussion literature where neuropsychological findings are concerned. Nonetheless, it is quite clear that research has led to the development of measures and indices that have wide-ranging influence in terms of assessing the validity of neuropsychological performance in various patient groups. The most obvious example is that of the FBS scale discussed above. Most of the work on the FBS originated in the context of head-injury–related forensic cases and has shown broad applicability to other clinical populations, particularly those involving prominent somatoform symptoms.

New ideas and measures are frequently met with resistance from seasoned clinicians who are accustomed to a certain mode of practice. Thus, while the development of various measures of symptom validity and effort has been intriguing, most clinicians blanch at the notion of administering interminable batteries of symptom validity tests. Fortunately, numerous "embedded" measures of effort have also emerged that can facilitate due diligence on the part of those practitioners who are not constantly involved in forensic assessment (Greiffenstein, Baker, & Gola, 1994; Larrabee, 2005b; Millis, Putnam, Adams, & Ricker, 1995; Mittenberg, Aguila-Puentes, Patton, Canyock, & Heilbronner, 2002; Sweet, 1999). The ingenuity of the neuropsychology community is a tremendous asset and one that will continue to assure the field's relevance.

Multiple Sclerosis/Autoimmune Disorders

Neuropsychologists often evaluate patients with a range of medical and neurological illness related to autoimmune dysfunction. The most common of these conditions is likely MS, which is an autoimmune inflammatory disease resulting in CNS demyelination (Bruck & Stadelmann, 2005). Neuropsychological deficits associated with MS are well known and include difficulties with processing speed, attention, working memory, and executive abilities (Benedict et al., 2006; Bobholz & Rao, 2003; Rao, Leo, Bernardin, & Unverzagt, 1991). Nevertheless, MS can present in extremely variable ways, and it would be dubious to assert that there is a prototypical cognitive presentation in MS. In addition to the cognitive difficulties seen in MS, a number of common physical and psychological symptoms tend to overlap those reported in CFS, fibromyalgia, MCS, and NES. The most prominent physical symptom noted clinically in MS patients is fatigue, though patients also experience pain, dizziness, numbness, gait problems, and depression. As such, MS has frequently been used as a neurological comparison sample in studies examining neuropsychological functioning in the various conditions noted above (Daly, Komaroff, Bloomingdale, Wilson, & Albert, 2001; DeLuca et al., 1993; DeLuca, Johnson, Beldowicz, & Natelson, 1995; Johnson, DeLuca, Diamond, & Natelson, 1996, 1998; Krupp, Sliwinski, Masur, & Friedberg, 1994; van der Werf, Prins, Jongen, van der Meer, & Bleijenberg, 2000).

A few different patterns of performance have been noted in these studies, though it is not clear whether they relate to sample characteristics, the nature of tasks examined, or the degree of neuropsychiatric symptomatology. Studies have attempted to control for some of these elements, but none typically did so in a comprehensive way. Several studies indicated that cognitive difficulties were similar in CFS and MS patient groups, with both groups showing impairment relative to controls (Daly et al., 2001; DeLuca et al., 1993; Johnson et al. 1998). Others indicated that CFS patients showed greater impairment than MS patients and controls on some tasks (DeLuca et al., 1995; Johnson, DeLuca, Diamond, & Natelson, 1996), and one study showed that MS patients evidence greater cognitive difficulties than do CFS patients (Krupp et al., 1994). One report examined performance of MS and CFS patients on a forced-choice symptom validity measure (van der Werf et al., 2000). These authors found that 30% of the CFS group showed suspect effort as compared to 13% of the MS group. Importantly, overall performance of patient groups did not differ on neuropsychological measures, with both groups showing impairment in just greater than 15% of the sample. This underscores the importance of assessing effort in such studies, because similarities and differences in clinical groups might well change if level of effort is considered (Drane et al., 2006).

Another focus of studies comparing CFS and MS patients has been to examine scores on various symptom, personality, and psychopathology measures (Christodoulou et al., 1999; Dendy, Cooper, & Sharpe, 2001; Johnson, DeLuca, & Natelson, 1996a, 1996b, 1996c; Johnson, Lange, Tiersky, DeLuca, & Natelson, 2001; Pepper, Krupp, Friedberg, & Doscher, 1993; Taillefer, Kirmayer, Robbins, & Lasry, 2002, 2003; Van Houdenhove et al., 2002). Not surprisingly, there is some variability in these findings, though many of the studies suggest that CFS and MS patients share a number of characteristics when compared to normal controls. These features include mildly elevated depressive symptomatology (Johnson, DeLuca, & Natelson, 1996c), higher harm avoidance and lower reward dependence (Christodoulou et al., 1999), greater alexithymia and depressive attributional style (Johnson et al., 2001), less self-reproach (Johnson, DeLuca, & Natelson, 1996a), and less depression and fewer personality disorders compared to depressed subjects (Pepper et al., 1993). A few studies indicated greater difficulty or pathology for CFS versus MS patients, including illness worry, greater fatigue and lower functional status (Taillefer et al., 2002, 2003), and more "hassles" and higher emotional difficulties and pain (Van Houdenhove et al., 2002).

Thus, while it appears that MS patients have been used as a neurological control group for functional somatic syndromes, it also appears that patients with MS and other autoimmune disorders are prone to reporting high levels of physical symptomatology. The typical clinical attribution for these problems is that the physical and psychological adjustment issues relate directly to the CNS disease process, though it would also stand to reason that, within the population of MS and other autoimmune disorder patients, there are those more prone to somatoform disorders based on a multitude of factors, as discussed in chapter 4.

The methodology in a recent study by Carone, Benedict, Munschauer, Fishman, and Weinstock-Guttman (2005) may provide an interesting take on this general question. In this study, a large group of MS patients and informants completed the Multiple Sclerosis Neuropsychological Questionnaire (Benedict et al., 2003). Patients were distributed into groups based on the discrepancy between their own ratings of symptomatology and the ratings of an informant. Carone et al. (2005) found that MS patients who overestimated their cognitive abilities were less depressed, less conscientious, more disinhibited, more euphoric, and more typically disabled. "Underestimators" were typically more depressed, though they showed little in the way of cognitive deficits relative to patients who accurately estimated their cognitive impairment. While these results do not directly speak to the issue of somatoform symptoms in MS, it is possible that this methodology could identify those whose cognitive and physical complaints might be considered overestimated by a more objective standard.

Within a typical neuropsychological assessment practice, it is also possible that somatizing patients with legitimate neurological disease are referred more frequently by virtue of the nature and frequency of their complaints. A case example of such a patient with multiple autoimmune disorder indicators is presented in chapter 7. As with all of the other conditions and diagnoses discussed in this chapter, methodologies to assess symptom validity can be employed in studies with patients with autoimmune disorders. While some might question the wisdom of, in essence, "not trusting" patients with "real" diseases, there is good reason to use such measures to validate what we believe we know about neuropsychological functioning in these disorders. Further, establishing a database that addresses performance of a wide range of patient groups on measures that are thought to assess effort, motivation, and overreporting of symptoms is simply a good idea. I could identify only one peer-reviewed study directly examining FBS, WMT, TOMM, or other neuropsychological measures of symptom validity and effort with patients with autoimmune disorders (van der Werf et al., 2000). Of course, this is likely to change with an increased emphasis on the validation of these measures outside of the forensic context. This will be helpful in identifying appropriate clinical cut-offs for samples with known medical and neurological disease.

Summary

While somatoform symptoms and disorders have been described for many years, evaluation tools for the assessment of the psychological and neuro-psychological aspects of these syndromes have only recently evolved to a point where we can accurately capture their essence. Cataloguing and describing symptoms are very important and help clinicians to understand and identify various presentations, but neuropsychological assessment and the insights of neuropsychologists have been particularly helpful in advancing diagnostic accuracy. As discussed in chapter 2, somatoform illnesses evolve as a function of increased technological understanding and general sophistication of diagnostic methods (Shorter, 1992). Like neuroimaging, EEG, and other technologies, current neuropsychological measures are helping to bring somatoform syndromes into a different light, improving conceptualization and treatment and moving us closer to a goal of a less dualistic system of understanding neuropsychiatric illness.

In a sense, symptom validity measures, including performance related measures (e.g., PDRT, TOMM, WMT), embedded measures of symptom validity, and specialized validity indices from standard personality measures (e.g., FBS, HHI, RBS), may well represent the technology that helps to move the current set of somatoform disorders into a different realm of understanding. In chapter 6, I review literature examining various treatment strategies for somatoform disorders. Recent research has identified more comprehensive ways of working with somatizing patients that acknowledge the importance of emotional recognition and affect regulation. While the task may seem daunting, progress in treatment approaches is clearly being made.

6

Management of Somatoform Disorders

The Context of Psychological Management of Somatoform Disorders

Neuropsychologists practicing in the United States tend to devote little of their time to psychotherapy or treatment, though they frequently make recommendations for treatment as part of the neuropsychological evaluation process. More than 45% of all neuropsychologists responding to a recent wide-scale survey acknowledged that they did no psychotherapy with patients without brain dysfunction. The average amount of time spent engaging in psychotherapy across all respondents and settings, and encompassing patients with and without acquired brain dysfunction, was about seven hours per week (Sweet, Peck, Abramowitz, & Etzweiler, 2002). This does not necessarily mean seven hours of psychotherapy, but rather seven hours in the provision of these services. Thus, despite the fact that the vast majority of neuropsychologists are trained in clinical psychology programs, the nature of neuropsychological practice is such that treatment and psychotherapy are decidedly secondary pursuits (Sweet et al., 2002; Sweet, Nelson, & Moberg, 2006). Clinical neuropsychology has instead staked its reputation on the ability to accurately characterize neurobehavioral functioning. Ideally, such a focus encompasses a ready knowledge of the most appropriate and efficacious treatments for our patients.

Biases

For most traditionally trained neuropsychologists, there tend to be a number of clinical pearls of wisdom about somatizing patients that are passed on in a fairly immutable fashion. First, somatizing patients are lacking in insight and are "brittle" with respect to understanding the essence of their problems. Second, as a result of their lack of insight, they are poor prospects for psychotherapy, particularly insight-oriented therapies. Third, the best that can typically be done for somatizing patients is to pharmacologically treat symptoms of mood and/or anxiety disorders with the hope that this will provide some general relief. Ultimately, somatizing patients are considered difficult to treat because of their lack of willingness to acknowledge the psychological nature of their problems (Graham, 2006). These beliefs reflect a bias that is not specific to clinical neuropsychology, though it underscores the fact that somatizing patients are challenging on many levels. While neuropsychologists are likely to cite relevant literature or factual data in arriving at the above conclusions (Allen, Escobar, Lehrer, Gara, & Woolfolk, 2002), the difficult personality features of somatizing patients can also affect clinicians' interest in working with them in less obvious ways. Intuitively, it seems that this patient group may be particularly vulnerable to adversely affecting their own care by virtue of some of their more disagreeable personality features.

In the broader clinical and social psychology literature, many studies look at the nature of biases held in interpersonal interactions and, more specifically, in the process of treatment and assessment (Aklin and Turner, 2006; Frith & Frith, 2006; Raine, Carter, Sensky, & Black, 2004; Wood, Romero, Knutson, & Grafman, 2005). These studies range from basic comparisons of practitioner attitudes about patients with functional somatic syndromes (FSSs; Raine et al., 2004) to studies that assess "attitudes" in a way that only neuroscientists might appreciate (Wood et al., 2005). The general message is that attitudes and biases about patients are multidetermined and not necessarily accurate. There is no reason to assume that neuropsychologists are any more or less prone to being affected by such biases, though as professionals who often represent the "entry point" to psychological services, one might argue that special care needs to be exercised in not betraying any negative biases that might exist. As with many things in life, some considerable reflection on one's feelings and biases about patients is always worthwhile (Williams & Day, 2007).

Psychosomatic Medicine

Working with patients who are challenging on so many different levels is not for the timid. Many clinicians and researchers even regard such patients as worthy tests of their ability to develop and provide effective treatments. It would seem that this was the spirit in which "psychosomatic medicine" emerged as a subspecialty area about 70 years ago. With the publication of the journal *Psychosomatic Medicine* in 1939 and a textbook several years later (Weiss & Spurgeon, 1943), the American Psychosomatic Society was born. Some 65 years later, in 2005, the American Board of Psychiatry and Neurology designated psychosomatic medicine as an area of subspecialty certification. Typically, descriptions of psychosomatic medicine have been quite broad and include "the diagnosis and treatment of psychiatric disorders in complex medically ill patients" (ABPN, 2008). This subspecialty encompasses what has traditionally been called *consultation liaison psychiatry*, including working with patients with somatoform disorders. Given the breadth of this subspecialty area, it is not surprising that the amount of treatment research involving somatization and somatoform disorders has been modest compared to other neuropsychiatric disorders. Nevertheless, professional journals with a psychosomatic medicine focus have provided a good fit for studies examining somatizing patients.

Psychosomatic medicine and psychology have long maintained that interactions between mind (i.e., consciousness) and body are complex but basically inseparable. *Descartes' Error* was not discovered with the publication of Antonio R. Damasio's book in 1994, but rather by many clinicians and researchers before and since Descartes' mind–body dualism became a dominant philosophical stance in the mid-1600s. To most clinicians with even the most basic neuroscience foundation, the notion of a mind or consciousness being separate from the sublime activities of the brain seems fundamentally absurd. Neuroscientists believe in a broad sense that consciousness is a product of the brain and its complex workings. If we believe that consciousness is a product of the CNS, it is not much of a leap to imagine that psychological symptoms or stressors emanate from the brain and, further, that many physical sensations might well also come primarily from the workings of the brain.

The experience of pain is instructive and compelling in that it has been shown to be mediated by different regions of the brain, and that it is responsive to both pharmacological and psychological treatments. Pain and somatoform symptoms are literally "in one's head," because without the brain to interpret pain information, there would be no experience of pain. Further, psychologically oriented treatments (i.e., psychotherapy) are therefore understandable as methods that change brain function. The morphing of psychological science into brain science was important as a conduit between mind and body. Neuropsychology and neuroscience played no small role in this transformation, and some of the models and approaches discussed in chapter 4 seized the opportunity to bring together psychological and biological means of understanding and treating clinical problems.

Approaches to Management

The contemporary literature examining treatment methods for somatoform disorders is modest in terms of the number of randomized controlled studies (Allen et al., 2002; Woolfolk & Allen, 2007). Because many such studies came from the psychosomatic medicine literature, they have focused on syndromes that do not correspond directly to *DSM*-based somatoform disorders (i.e., FSSs). Further, behavioral and cognitive behavioral treatments have been examined with a much greater frequency because these treatments gained popularity in the later part of the twentieth century. The methodology of cognitive behavior therapy (CBT) and behavior therapy approaches tends to be more regimented and, as a result, easier to incorporate in larger scale studies. However, because of the complexity of somatoform disorders and the wide range of problematic symptoms, most treatment studies employ multiple methods, as discussed in the next section.

In chapter 4, a number of developmental theories were discussed as models for understanding the emergence of somatoform disorders in a given individual. Each of the developmental viewpoints proposes an etiology and, by association, suggests possible treatment approaches. Developmental theories are by their nature broad and inclusive. They attempt to account for a wide range of behavior and psychopathology. In contrast, treatments may vary widely depending upon what specific symptoms are to be managed. Psychodynamic theories tend to be more encompassing in terms of treatment goals, while behavioral treatments often focus on very specific behaviors. Both approaches are important in treating somatizing patients. For example, a psychoanalytically oriented therapist might spend a good deal of time trying to help a patient understand patterns of interactions in important relationships and how that might lead to discomfort, fear, or neurotic behavior. In contrast, a behaviorally oriented therapist might focus on a particular problematic behavior and develop a very specific program to reduce or eliminate that behavior. Both approaches have merit, and both can be used without concern about defiling the method of the other. In their book *Treating Somatization*, Woolfolk and Allen (2007) emphasize the fact many treatment approaches borrow from different theoretical perspectives.

When the scope of treatment research is broadened, the nature of the clinical issues might also change substantially. For instance, work examining treatment of hypochondriasis or "health anxiety" is relevant because it over-laps with many of the clinical issues encountered in working with somatizing patients (Taylor & Asmundson, 2004). Also, behavioral and cognitive behavioral treatment methods for pain management have been widely studied for more than 30 years (Fordyce et al., 1973; Hoffman, Papas, Chatkoff, & Kerns, 2007). The nonspecific nature of symptoms in somatization disorder has made systematic and theoretically focused study difficult. The clinical reality calls for approaching treatment in a way that allows multiple symptoms to be addressed with the most appropriate and efficacious treatments. Thus, knowledge of treatment approaches and disorders beyond somatization and somatoform disorders is important.

Treatment literature on somatoform disorders can be organized by syndrome or by treatment approach. Most of the well-controlled studies done in the past 10 years have focused on one of the FSSs (e.g., fibromyalgia, chronic fatigue syndrome [CFS]) or clinically defined variants of somatization (e.g., abridged somatization, multisomatoform disorder). Because the FSSs are a bit more specific in terms of definition and range of symptoms, these have provided a more focused opportunity for treatment research. Further, the focus on physical symptoms in FSSs has led to the routine use of a number of non-psychological interventions. Relaxation and exercise are most often used in studies treating irritable bowel syndrome (IBS), fibromyalgia, and CFS (Whorwell, Prior, & Farragher, 1984; Wearden et al., 1998; Martin et al., 1996). In this context, these interventions make good sense and are often shown to be helpful relative to standard medical care.

For this discussion, I focus on psychotherapy-based treatments as they pertain to relevant somatoform disorders. This is a growing literature with a number of well-conducted studies over the past several years (Allen, Woolfolk, Escobar, Gara, & Hamer, 2006; Woolfolk & Allen, 2007).

Cognitive Behavior Therapy Approaches

CBT approaches have emerged as the most widely researched and utilized for FSSs and somatoform disorders. CBT for somatization is based on the idea that patients are troubled by how they think about events and symptoms. The basic goal of CBT for FSS/somatization is to challenge and change the dysfunctional thoughts and behaviors related to a patient's somatoform symptoms. A small number of reviews have described varied results with CBT in somatoform disorders and FSSs (Allen et al., 2002; Kroenke & Swindle, 2000; Tazaki & Landlaw, 2006; Woolfolk & Allen, 2007). It is beyond the scope of this chapter to discuss all of the studies involved in these summaries, or even to update all of the relevant studies since the publication of reviews cited. However, there has been impressive growth in the number and quality of studies examining CBT in somatization, and this trend will likely continue as the value of management of these patients becomes increasingly clear (Hiller, Fichter, & Rief, 2003; Sumathipala, Hewege, Hanwella, & Mann, 2000).

An early review examined studies that focused exclusively on CBT approaches with somatoform disorders. While methodologies and outcome measures were variable, it was reported that more than 80% of included studies indicated improvement (or a trend toward improvement) in reported physical functioning following treatment. In contrast, 46% of studies showed improvement or a trend (decline) in psychological distress, and 26% of the studies suggested that CBT helped to improve functional status or skills (Kroenke & Swindle, 2000). This is an intriguing finding that highlights some interesting dynamics in terms of the nature of complaints and outcome measures used in different studies. It may be that somatizing patients' defenses are such that they can acknowledge physical improvement in the "physical" disorders they have, while reporting psychological improvement might involve too much of an acknowledgment of the "mental" aspects of their disorder.

Randomized controlled studies of various psychosocial treatments, ranging from exercise and relaxation to short-term psychodynamic psychotherapy and CBT, were reviewed by Allen et al. (2002). This review was organized by clinical disorder and included studies examining a range of treatments for somatization disorder, IBS, CFS, and fibromyalgia. These researchers construed the various patient groups as "polysymptomatic somatizers," emphasizing the fact that most patients with these labels have multiple symptoms and substantial overlap of physical symptomatology. Further, there is overlap in the psychological features of these disorders, which makes comparisons of treatment approaches relevant. Overall, there were no substantial differences in how polysymptomatic somatizers responded to various treatments. CBT showed mixed results, with significant reduction in reported symptoms in some studies and no significant difference between CBT and other treatment conditions and controls (Allen et al., 2002).

In one study examining patients with five or more unexplained physical symptoms, CBT was compared to standard medical care. Patients who received six 30-minute sessions of CBT had greater reductions in health care visits and physical complaints than a standard medical care group of somatizing patients (Sumathipala et al., 2000). Another study looked at health care utilization as a measure of the effectiveness of CBT in patients with somatoform disorders. Individuals who received CBT showed markedly decreased utilization, as well as lower indirect socioeconomic costs, relative to a waiting list control (Hiller et al., 2003). The above-noted effect of CBT on physical symptom report (Kroenke & Swindle, 2000) was reiterated in an unpublished study involving a large sample of Latino patients who were given CBT. It was once again noted that CBT reduced physical symptom reporting relative to psychiatric symptom reporting (Lamberg, 2005). Finally, a recent randomized controlled trial with somatization disorder patients showed that patients who were given a ten-session, manualized CBT program maintained improvements in symptom report, self-reported functioning, and health care costs relative to a standard medical care comparison sample at 15 months posttreatment (Allen et al., 2006). Thus, as CBT regimens become more standardized and focused on somatization, it would appear that positive findings are more consistently obtained and of a greater magnitude.

Results in studies examining CBT for IBS are mixed. This is likely due to the wide-ranging methodologies and the fact that most studies incorporate some kind of relaxation or biofeedback component. Therefore, it is difficult to parse the relative effects of CBT versus relaxation or other more specific methods. Further, the symptomatology of IBS is arguably more focused (on the gastro-intestinal system) than that noted for somatization disorder, CFS, or fibro-myalgia (Allen et al., 2002; Woolfolk & Allen, 2007). A recent study showed positive benefit of CBT relative to a trycyclic antidepressant, an educational group, and a placebo (Drossman et al., 2003). In contrast, no group differences were noted among CBT, relaxation, and standard medical care with a relaxation component in another recent study (Boyce, Talley, Balaam, Koloski, & Truman, 2003). It may be that IBS symptoms are more amenable to such interventions as relaxation training and biofeedback, and IBS patients may not be characterized by as much general psychopathology as are patients with other FSSs.

Treatment studies of patients with CFS have shown similar variability in outcome as measured by fatigue ratings. A recent summary of CBT studies for CFS (Woolfolk & Allen, 2007) indicated that one study showed no beneficial effect of CBT, while three others indicated reduced fatigue in patients who were given CBT versus other kinds of treatments, such as relaxation and support groups. One study indicated that the advantage seen in CBT was maintained up to five years after treatment (Deale, Husain, Chalder, & Wessely, 2001), while another study showed lower cost and greater effectiveness of CBT relative to support groups and "natural course" groups (Severens, Prins, van der Wilt, van der Meer, & Bleijenberg, 2004). Woolfolk and Allen (2007) remarked that the level of intensity of CBT treatments along with improvements in study methodologies has resulted in more positive results in CBT with CFS samples.

For whatever reason, CBT studies examining fibromyalgia patients have generally studied group approaches and have not been impressive (Allen et al., 2002; Woolfolk & Allen, 2007). It seems likely that group approaches are more palatable to individuals diagnosed with fibromyalgia. That is, support and educationally oriented groups are common in various FSSs and therefore offer a therapeutic "foot in the door." Nevertheless, CBT and educationally oriented groups tended not to have much of an effect on pain complaints, pain intensity, or activity levels (Allen et al., 2002). The nature of complaints in fibromyalgia (i.e., muscle soreness, pain) also means that patients are typically referred from more specialized rheumatology practices, and the choice of treatments is likely influenced by the professionals participating. Despite the fact that CBT has been a popular approach, studies employing a well-standardized and individualized treatment approach are rare.

In summary, CBT seems to enjoy the status of a treatment modality that various professionals see as accessible and reasonable. That is, the ability to specify a certain number of visits, specific content to be covered, and a fairly simple overriding set of principles (identifying and changing dysfunctional cognitions) seems a sensible approach. The implementation of strong CBT programs has been a challenge because of the nature of different referral settings. Primary care, gastroenterology, and rheumatology clinics are all likely able to appreciate the benefit of CBT to their patients. Whether they are able to adequately implement such programs is another matter. Going forth, it will be critical to specify the structure and implementation of CBT programs, like that described by Woolfolk and Allen (2007). Even given the extremely variable nature of CBT interventions described in the literature over the past 10 years, results are promising.

Psychodynamic Approaches
Psychodynamically oriented theories about somatization view somatoform symptoms as a means for allowing emotional trauma to be experienced in a less threatening or frightening manner. As such, the goals of psychodynamic psychotherapy involve facilitating the understanding of what underlies an individual's (physical) symptoms. This is accomplished through a typically lengthy process in which a therapeutic alliance is established via free associ-

ation, with eventual interpretation of the transference. The psychoanalytic method is by its nature protracted and full of nuance, and this has been a major obstacle to standardizing and studying its techniques. In contrast, short-term dynamic therapy emerged in the 1960s and 1970s as a method for taking advantage of the theoretical richness of ego psychology and attachment theory in a more intense and expeditious manner (Davanloo, 1995; Sifneos, 1987). These techniques grew out of hospital and academic psychiatry settings where there was a clear need to affect change in a briefer time span than the several years that was often required in a typical analysis.

Aside from scattered case studies, there is little compelling empirical work assessing the value of psychodynamic therapy approaches in the treatment of somatization. The exceptions have been a number of studies conducted with IBS patients (Creed et al., 2003, 2005; Guthrie, Creed, Dawson, & Tomenson, 1991; Svedlund, Sjodin, Ottosson, & Dotevall, 1983). An early study examined 101 patients who were randomly assigned to either a standard medical care group or a group that received 10 hour-long sessions of "dynamically oriented individual psychotherapy," in addition to standard medical care. The psychotherapy treatment group showed significantly less somatic symptomatology both three months and one year posttreatment. The difference between groups after one year was greater than it was immediately following treatment, suggesting a strong and lasting effect of therapy (Svedlund, 1983; Svedlund et al., 1983). A similar study was reported by the same group a few years later, this time studying patients with peptic ulcer disease. It is not clear whether these were the same or overlapping patient groups, but the results were reported to be essentially the same (Sjodin, Svedlund, Ottosson, & Dotevall, 1986). Another group has reported several studies examining dynamically oriented therapy with IBS patients (Creed et al., 2003, 2005; Guthrie et al., 1991), with similar positive results. In these studies, treatment included therapy that focused on the relationship between emotions and IBS symptoms, as well as relaxation training and standard medical treatment. One of the studies examined the cost-effectiveness of psychotherapy and paroxetine relative to standard medical care (Creed et al., 2003). The authors found that health care costs in the year following treatment were lowest for patients in the psychotherapy group, second lowest for the paroxetine group, and highest for standard medical care. These kinds of results mirror those reported in the CBT treatment literature, albeit in a much more specific context.

As with the CBT approaches described above, short-term dynamic therapy approaches are often used along with ancillary methods involving relaxation, education, and other professionals in different professional contexts. It has become clear that there are considerable benefits to a focused and programmatic approach to working with such patients. The benefits are increasingly being demonstrated in the economic context, which, for better or worse, will likely be the prevailing standard in the future.

Integrative Treatment Approaches

To a significant extent, the CBT and dynamic therapy treatment studies discussed are integrative. That is, instead of adhering rigidly to a specific psychotherapy model or philosophy, researchers and clinicians are picking and choosing elements of other therapies that are known to improve effectiveness. For instance, psychodynamically oriented treatments are incorporating more structure and time limits because these facilitate improvement in patients, given typical treatment environments and constraints. Similarly, CBT-oriented treatments are incorporating more discussion and processing of emotion and interpersonal content because this important material is often neglected in more structured therapy approaches. The end result is that there are fewer "typical" kinds of therapies being utilized with somatizing patients.

Interpersonal Psychotherapy

Another example of a therapy approach that integrates many different perspectives is interpersonal psychotherapy (IPT). This approach focuses on problems in interpersonal relationships and how these relate to individuals' attachment needs. It is a "dynamically informed" psychotherapy with a general goal of improving interpersonal relationships and/or changing expectations about those relationships. Thus, rather than focusing on specific symptoms or behaviors, IPT emphasizes the importance of relationships and how individuals' needs are met through them (Stuart, 2006). In somatization, insecurely attached individuals use physical symptoms to convey their needs to others, often resulting in dysfunctional communication (Stuart & Noyes, 2006). Like short-term dynamic therapy, IPT is typically time limited, and like CBT, it is manual based and focused on specific techniques. IPT is based on attachment theory and, as such, integrates a number of different ways of thinking about behavior and relationships. There is not an artificial limiting of symptoms to be treated or issues to be discussed, but rather a focus on improving that which is thought to underlie all forms of pathology, difficulties in interpersonal relationships. There is little in the clinical literature examining

IPT with somatizing patients, though there is mounting interest (Stuart, 2006; Stuart & Noyes, 2006).

Multimodality Approaches

The other kind of integration that occurs involves the range of treatment modalities. Most treatment trials with somatizing patients include interventions that go well beyond traditional psychotherapy. The minimum standard in most studies is that all participants get typical medical care, which is not without its nuance and variability. When psychotherapy, relaxation, exercise, and educational components are added to treatment approaches, it becomes very difficult to identify the "active ingredient" in treatment efficacy. The whole is clearly greater than the sum of its parts, because most programs are more interested in providing effective and helpful services than they are demonstrating the relative contribution of one elements of treatment versus another.

Affective Cognitive Behavioral Therapy

Affective cognitive behavioral therapy (ACBT) is the moniker given to the treatment program described by Woolfolk and Allen in their 2007 book *Treating Somatization: A Cognitive-Behavioral Approach*. This extensive and integrative approach is the product of years of experience and two peer-reviewed studies with somatizing patients (Allen, Woolfolk, Lehrer, Gara, & Escobar, 2001; Allen et al., 2006). The book includes a manual for conducting a 10-session CBT program, an abbreviated program for progressive muscle relaxation, a symptom severity scale, a somatic symptom questionnaire, and a list of questions to encourage examination of cognitions.

Woolfolk and Allen (2007) acknowledge that there are many elements of their approach that have evolved and many elements that are not likely to be adequately addressed in a 10-session program. Prominent among these are issues with emotional awareness and interpersonal relationships. They comment,

> Training in emotional awareness and labeling of affect was a component of the original 10-session version of this treatment. We came to believe that, in order to be implemented effectively and used in conjunction with cognitive methods in a comprehensive program of emotional regulation, the emotion focused methods should be expanded and made more central to the treatment. Also, in the 10-session version of the treatment, the various cognitive and behavioral techniques are implemented

---

adequately, but the therapeutic attack on the sick role tends to be preliminary and rather limited, as is the case with our attempts in that format to make patients emotionally self-aware. (p. 110)

They concluded that "the current, expanded treatment necessitates a more substantial and closer therapist-patient relationship than usually can be established in 10 sessions and, thus, assumes a longer period of contact between patient and therapist" (pp. 110–111).

Further, certain therapist characteristics are identified as ideal and are acknowledged as rare in the experiences of the authors. Not surprisingly, therapists with only a CBT background tend to struggle with the portions of the program that deal with distinguishing between thoughts and emotions. Woolfolk and Allen (2007) suggest that narrowly trained individuals struggle with "emotional nuance" and facilitating patients' experience of their emotions.

The acknowledgement of these limitations is important in that it allows others seeking to implement programs to understand the difficulty and complexity of the enterprise. Going forth, successful programs will need to integrate a wide range of techniques and employ highly skilled therapists and technicians in order to assure optimal results.

The Future of Treatment for Somatization

As recently as 15–20 years ago, there was little in the way of an organized presentation of ideas about how to treat patients with functional somatic symptoms. A group of clinicians and researchers interested in FSSs and their treatment convened a conference in Oxford, U.K., in 1992. Their efforts resulted in the book *Treatment of Functional Somatic Symptoms* (Mayou, Bass, & Sharpe, 1995), which covers conceptual, historical, and epidemiological aspects of functional somatic symptoms and disorders. The book was compiled to provide "a comprehensive account of the treatment of functional somatic symptoms. . . . " In the time that has elapsed since this publication, many studies have been conducted and many different conceptual models proposed. This chapter has reviewed much of this work as it relates to psychotherapeutic approaches, but to say that significant advances have been made would be a bit of an overstatement. The recent work by Woolfolk and Allen (2007) is a hopeful example of what can be accomplished with a careful analytical approach that is flexible and appreciative of the contributions of many different professionals working with these complex patients.

Whether there is a future for coordinated programs to treat somatization patients seems unclear at present. Specific programs for various FSSs are relatively common, and pain management programs and clinical practices are present in most urban areas and within large health care systems. The overlap between pain management programs and treatment programs for somatization/FSSs could be substantial. Psychologists' efforts in chronic pain management have been considerable, and they are a standard part of most pain management programs. The efficacy of psychotherapy methods is well established (Hoffman et al., 2007), and the inclusion of psychologists and psychological methods in interdisciplinary pain programs is also a standard (Stanos, McLean, & Rader, 2007). As mentioned above, the bottom line for the development of comprehensive programs for management of complex patients is increasingly an economic one. The impetus for development of multidisciplinary programs for treating FSSs will need to come, first, from a realization of the cost of treating these patients and, second, from a clear demonstration that there is an economic benefit of doing so in a more co-ordinated fashion (Allen et al., 2006; Creed et al., 2003; Severens et al., 2004). For the moment, there is a greater burden on individuals who refer patients for these services to educate themselves about local resources on a more individualized level.

7

Working With Somatizing Patients in Neuropsychological Practice

In this chapter I present composite case examples that illustrate different elements of working with somatizing patients in the context of the neuropsychological evaluation process. I start by discussing features of somatizing patients that are frequently encountered in practice. This material will likely seem familiar to most practitioners. The observations and suggestions offered are based on my knowledge of the literature, but more so on extensive experience in working with such patients. This can be a decidedly trial-and-error process and one in which the clinician frequently learns from mistakes and missteps.

How Somatizing Patients Present

Understanding that all clinical practices are different, I venture a description of two primary somatizing presentations, *stoic* and *expressive*, and provide some detail to flesh out these presentations. I return to the examples as I discuss different elements of the neuropsychological evaluation process. These basic presentations are noted by Woolfolk and Allen (2007) while traditionally others have focused on emotionally reactive features (Shapiro, 1965) or more emotionally restricted presentations (Taylor, Bagby, & Parker, 1997; Lane Sechrest, Shapiro, & Kaszniak, 2000). While stoic and expressive somatizing types are not fully validated in the research literature, there is ample heuristic value. Further, despite how differently these patients present clinically, their foundations are assumed to be very similar.

The Stoic Pattern—"Ms. D."

The first kind of somatizing patient tends to be referred by practitioners from various medical specialties such as neurology, rheumatology, infectious disease, and cardiology. They also come from primary care (family practice, internal medicine) clinics, chiropractic practices, and concerned family members. These patients appear stoic and matter-of-fact in conveying their concerns, and they emphasize the objective and medical nature of their problems. Often, there has been an event (an accident or injury), and the patient is simply not functioning at a level that is characteristic of them. While it is not universally true, the stoic patient tends to have had less overall contact with the medical system than the expressive patient. In fact, it may be the case that many expressive cases start out stoically and evolve as a function of frustration with "the system." It is important to note that all manner of combinations of symptoms, histories, and developmental courses are possible and that these specifics have yet to be researched extensively. Again, the heuristic value is emphasized in this discussion.

Stoic patients tend to be characterized by a rigid and obsessive personality style. It is not uncommon for these patients to be quite specific about when their difficulties started. They convey a sense that their whole world was turned upside down when they found out what their diagnosis was or immediately after an accident occurred. It is difficult to sort through the reality of such assertions because the stoic patient will have incorporated the historical truth of their experience in a way that makes it unassailable in their mind. In neuropsychology practices, the prototypical example of this presentation is the modal mild traumatic brain injury case. Patients will often state that "everything was fine" or that they "were perfectly healthy" before they sustained their injury. The pattern is similar, though perhaps less obvious to the examiner when the identified event is the proffering of a diagnosis. The dramatic and almost literary quality of "life changing in an instant" seems to be the main emotional hook for the stoic patient. To the extent that any emotion is shown, it is when discussing the event. "I didn't ask for this" or "this is not me" are oft-repeated themes that sometimes bring a brief, almost controlled outburst of emotions. It is as if the evidence presented is so clear that even the stoic patient can allow himself a moment of pure affect. The following case captures several elements of a typical stoic patient presentation.

Ms. D. was a 29-year-old biomedical engineer who worked in high-tech industry for a large medical manufacturing company. She described herself as a very hard working and committed student who made straight A's in her undergraduate studies. Upon graduating, she was offered a position as a junior engineer with a very good starting salary, and she decided to defer graduate training to take advantage of the opportunity. Ms. D. performed well in her first year on the job but did not advance in her career much beyond her initial job description. Within a year of starting her job, complaints of muscle soreness and stiffness emerged, and the patient struggled with intense pains in her neck and shoulders. She initially saw an orthopedic surgeon, who did a full workup. The surgeon found no cervical spine abnormalities and no indications for surgical intervention, and the patient was referred back to her primary care physician. Ms. D.'s internist prescribed a number of nonopiate analgesic and anti-inflammatory medications with little benefit. When the patient began to develop "migraine" headaches a number of different triptans were tried with little benefit. Ms. D. consulted with a chiropractor and began twice-weekly visits for adjustments and massage. She was subsequently referred to a rheumatologist by her primary care doctor. Within two years of starting her job, Ms. D. was diagnosed with fibromyalgia and was given an opiate analgesic (Darvocet) to use "as needed" when her pain became unbearable. While this medication helped with the worst of her symptoms, she became concerned that she was using too much medication and eventually determined that she would no longer take the narcotic medication.

Approximately two and a half years after starting her job, Ms. D. was involved in a motor vehicle accident that was alternately described by her primary care provided as a "fender bender" and by the patient as a "horrible rear end collision." What had been acceptable performance at work turned unacceptable, and Ms. D. reported unbearable pain and cognitive difficulty that made it impossible for her to meet her job demands. She was referred to a neurologist to assess these concerns and subsequently for a neuropsychological evaluation when no abnormalities were noted on MRI, EEG, and laboratory studies. The patient took a medical leave of absence roughly two weeks after attempting a return to work. When she was seen for the neuropsychological evaluation, she was approximately six months postaccident.

Ms. D. had no previous history of head trauma or other risk factors for neurological dysfunction. She saw her difficulties with concentration and attention as having emerged mainly since the car accident. While Ms. D. admitted that attention and concentration problems existed before the accident, the problems she experienced after the accident were fundamentally different and simply much worse. She came to believe that she must have hit her head in the accident and consequently must have lost consciousness, as well. It did not seem at all unusual to the patient that this "horrible" accident would have resulted in her current problems with cognitive functioning.

Stoic somatizers are often quite compelling to their primary care providers. Their straightforward and earnest presentation is often regarded as steely resolve that is archetypal and seemingly inspirational to many caregivers. These patients are often congratulated on their toughness and reassured that there will be a ready solution for their difficulties. It is hard for many clinicians to believe that there would not be a quick resolution or response to basic treatment.

The Expressive Pattern—"Mr. M."

In seeming contrast to the stoic pattern, some somatizing patients conform more to what was traditionally described as the hysterical personality style. These patients are characterized by histrionic personality features, depression and anxiety symptoms, hypersensitivity, and dramatic remonstrations with regard to their discomfort.

The "neurotic style" of hysteria offered by Shapiro (1965) is consistent with what had long been described in the psychodynamic literature. That is, hysterical or somatizing patients were prone to histrionics, flamboyance, and a vague cognitive style. Such patients are common in psychiatry and general mental health practices. In seeming opposition to the stoic patient, expressive patients make it abundantly clear that they are suffering. Their emotions are very near the surface, and it is sometimes difficult to get through interviews because of this. Expressive patients can be digressive because they are often sidetracked by details that remind them of other experiences and symptoms that are problematic, and very important. These patients will often take the initial "what brings you in?" query and run with it, making the litany of their complaints seem rehearsed and familiar. Often, the clinician will be struck by the patient's press to get in all the details before he or she is cut off or redirected. Inexperienced or exceedingly patient clinicians might well be subjected to an expansive narrative lasting half an hour or more. Often, however, expressive patients have a few symptoms and concerns that they regard as most significant and worrisome, at least in the context of the neuropsychological evaluation.

It is not unusual for patients to have conducted some considerable "research" on their various conditions and to regard themselves as experts. Expressive patients are often unabashedly intolerant of incompetent practitioners who are ignorant of their diagnoses and symptoms. Patients will frequently ask direct questions about the clinician's background with a specific diagnosis and give indications of their knowledge therein. They might also share their experiences with experts in the field or do some name-dropping, presumably to check for recognition and/or engage in subtle one-upmanship.

The following case provides an example of an expressive patient with a presenting complaint of increasing cognitive dysfunction following an exposure to gasoline in a work-related incident. The referral question had to do with whether this exposure was related to recent onset difficulties with attention and "short-term memory."

Mr. M. was a 46-year-old man who worked as a truck driver and dispatcher for a construction company. He was referred for evaluation by an occupational health physician who saw him after an incident involving the patient being doused with gasoline when filling up his truck. The handle on the gas pump apparently jammed and, as Mr. M. extracted the pump handle from his gas tank, it sprayed all over the front of him, getting in his face and eyes. He believes that he swallowed a small amount of gasoline and reports having vomited on the scene. He remembers feeling disoriented and dizzy, and he was taken to a washroom, where he rinsed himself off and washed out his mouth. A co-worker took him to an emergency department after he changed out of his work clothes. Mr. M. was examined in the emergency department and given some instructions regarding what to do if he experienced any further symptoms. He returned home and had a small meal before going to bed. The patient did not return to work the following day (a Friday) and returned to work on the following Monday. He reports that he continued to experience an upset stomach and dizziness.

Mr. M. found himself becoming dizzy and getting headaches when he was around gasoline fumes. He had more headaches in general and found that a number of other strong odors (e.g., cologne and nail polish remover) tended to make him dizzy and headachy. Over the next three months, the patient missed approximately three weeks of work secondary to these symptoms. In addition, he complained of problems with focus and concentration and felt subjectively that his "short-term" memory had declined. Mr. M. visited the company physician, who did some labwork and a couple of physical exams and found nothing wrong with patient. He referred him for a neuropsychological assessment, requesting evaluation of attention and concentration problems, but also noted Mr. M.'s somatoform tendencies.

During our initial contact, Mr. M. asked if I had any experience with "idiopathic environmental illness" or multiple chemical sensitivities. I told him that I had seen a number of patients with that clinical description over the years. He then asked if I "believed in it." I assured Mr. M. that I believe that all patients come in with symptoms that are troubling to them and that I take their concerns at face value. I told him that I preferred not to get into discussions about various symptoms and disorders because I had limited time to get to know him and understand what he was having trouble with. He protested weakly, explaining that he was not interested in wasting his time with a doctor who was not aware of the nuances of this "disease," but allowed me to move forward with the interview. While we began with his concerns about concentration and memory, Mr. M. quickly revealed that he was being treated for many other health concerns, including chronic low back pain, fibromyalgia, migraine headaches, irritable bowel syndrome, and depression. However, he stated that he had an excellent work record and had been with his current employer for eight years. Upon closer evaluation, he had been on short-term disability with his current employer three separate times in eight years and had four other short-term disability leaves of absence with other employers. These were typically related to low back problems, though one episode was because of a "nervous breakdown" during a divorce and another was due to intractable headaches. According to Mr. M., he had been terminated from two jobs because of his health issues. He initiated a lawsuit against one of these employers and was given a small settlement.

On several occasions, Mr. M. became tearful and angry when describing his experiences. He stated that he was always regarded as an exceptional worker and that he had never been sick a day in his life until he injured his back at the age of 26 when doing concrete work. In the 20 years since that injury, Mr. M. portrayed himself as a "trooper" working with pain and discomfort of a kind that would be devastating to most people. He had sought treatment from a wide range of professionals, including herbalists, chiropractors, acupuncturists, hypnotists, orthopedic surgeons, and a number of other medical specialists. Mr. M. had not sustained treatment with any of these individuals for more than one year, and he had never seen a psychologist or therapist. When asked about this, he angrily stated that these problems were not in his head and that he did not need a shrink who didn't know anything about real pain to tell him that he was crazy. He recanted and acknowledged having seen a therapist two times. Mr. M. said that all the therapists did was talk about their own problems and that they cried when he told them about his various illnesses and travails.

Were all the details of Mr. M.'s history to be included, it would go on for many pages. For the purposes of the neuropsychological evaluation, Mr. M. reported a number of blows to the head that he thought might be considered concussions. He reported two such incidents related to participation in high school sports, neither of which resulted in an emergency department visit or any care beyond what was delivered on the field. The patient also reported being hit on the head multiple times by his physically abusive father, though he does not recall ever having lost consciousness as a result. Mr. M. acknowledged occasional binge drinking—usually to manage unbearable pain. He denied any history of treatment for substance abuse issues. The patient believed, in retrospect, that he may have had a learning disorder and/or ADD because he "had all those symptoms" when he looked at a few different checklists on the Internet. When asked about the natural history of his cognitive symptoms, Mr. M. was adamant in stating that while he had many of these kinds of symptoms in the past, none of them was as bad as they currently were. In other words, despite the reported history, in the mind of Mr. M., the current issues were solely related to the gasoline exposure incident.

The Stoic–Expressive Continuum

Stoic and expressive somatizing presentations could be considered different ontogenetic forms within the somatizing patient. That is, the stoic presentation may be more common in early interactions with the health care system. Prohibitions about personal weakness are still prominent in this stage, and there is a general awareness that seeking a doctor's help is a significant acknowledgment of personal weakness. Thus, the stoic patient may well feel uncomfortable with seeking help in such a direct fashion. This does not mean that other forms of help seeking have not been attempted or even overutilized. For instance, in the early stages, somatizing patients may wear out their welcome with loved ones or relatives. They may complain at work or use nonprescription medicines excessively. By the time these patients come to the attention of the health care system, they may feel like they have tried everything in their power to affect some kind of therapeutic change. Often, somatizing patients experience a sense of liberation that they are going to achieve some relief or, better still, a cure. Most of the time, they simply do not. This dynamic is nicely captured in the typical somatization profile on the MMPI-2. That is, patients have multiple somatic complaints and limited insight into the nature of these symptoms. Early in their help-seeking experience, they are assured that there is a ready solution for their problems and are reinforced in the belief that the answers lie outside of their sphere of influence. That is, it is not them, their character, their effort, or their own personal limitations that has anything to do with their suffering. When stoic patients are not "cured," they are often encouraged to seek out another specialist, or are referred directly to one. The patients start to attribute their lack of progress to the incompetence of others or the complexity of their affliction. Providers come to understand in short order that these patients are simply not improving, and they may quickly, in the eyes of the patient, change their tune and place blame on the patients for not improving. This change of attitude and approach is very often off-putting to formerly stoic patients, who can become more dramatic or demanding in their presentation. They come to feel decidedly wronged, and they become more vocal in their self-advocacy. Before long, we have a more expressive or demanding presentation and the prospects for successful treatment would seem to be less positive as time passes.

In the following pages, I describe interactions with somatizing patients at various stages of the neuropsychological evaluation process. This is intended to provide some guidance regarding the facilitation of a smooth evaluation process, feedback, and eventual disposition of the patient.

Preevaluation

There is great variability in the conduct of neuropsychology practice (Lamberty, Courtney, & Heilbronner, 2003) and consequently many different ways to facilitate referrals and scheduling. Typically, a patient's initial contact with a neuropsychology practice is through their referring primary care provider or specialist. Somatizing patients, more so than other kinds of referrals, can be self-referred based on their personal research of their clinical problems. In my practice setting, patients are given appointments through a scheduling department without having much if any direct contact with the neuropsychology office/support staff. For the modal referral, this is efficient and straightforward. In some instances, referral sources or patients may want to contact our office directly to assure that they come prepared for the evaluation. Specific requests of this nature are sent to our department and handled by office staff and/or psychometrists. For some somatizing patients, there is a strong press to make contact and provide or seek out information about the upcoming assessment.

With the stoic somatizing patient, inquiries might be made in the spirit of making sure that the doctor has all relevant materials in advance of the appointment. The compulsive and rigid personality characteristics of some patients can actually be helpful because this allows a review of relevant information in advance of the assessment. On occasion, patients will request a brief phone conference with the neuropsychologist. Again, this is presented as a means of providing information, though often somatizing patients will seek to get some sense of the neuropsychologist's approach to assessment and any biases he or she might have. This is more typical of an expressive somatizing patient. The patients would like to convey that they are well informed about their diagnosis and clinical issues and would like to make sure that the doctor is equally so. The following is an example of a preevaluation contact with the somatizing patient:

> Ms. A. was a 36-year-old, married woman with a history of nonepileptic seizures (NESs). She contacted the office to speak with the doctor because there were some historical items she wanted to share. Ms. A. was concerned that some of this information would not be contained in the records that had already been sent to offices. The patient was assured that we had received a large packet of records and that the doctor would review these in advance of his meeting with her. Ms. A. was pleased to hear this but still wanted to speak with the doctor because she had some general questions about his background and experience with seizure disorder patients. She mentioned to office staff that she found general information on the American Psychological Association and American Academy of Clinical Neuropsychology Web sites, but that this did not provide acceptable background for her to make such a determination. Office staff passed this information on to the neuropsychologist, informing him that the patient would like to be called directly at her home number. Ms. A. called one additional time shortly after noon on the same day. Dr. L. returned her call later in the day to see if he could provide the information she was seeking. He provided her with some information about his training in epilepsy settings and apparently gave ample information regarding his knowledge of epilepsy and NES. The patient seemed satisfied and stated that she looked forward to her appointment (her fourth neuropsychological evaluation in seven years). Upon completion of the initial interview, Ms. A. requested a copy of Dr. L.'s curriculum vita, and this was provided.

The manner in which patients' requests for preevaluation phone conversations are handled is very much an issue of individual preference. Even with persistent patients, well-trained office staff can provide information in a way that will satisfy or discourage further attempts of most patients. That is, psychometrists or office managers who know their neuropsychologists well will be able to appease the demanding and curious somatizer.

Some neuropsychologists, particularly those who do a significant forensic or medicolegal practice, might reasonably determine that they will have no direct contact with the patient, for a number of reasons. Because the attorney or insurance carrier is technically the client in these arrangements, there is good cause to refuse contacts with patients until the evaluation meeting. In most such cases, neuropsychologists are provided with all information to be considered in conducting their evaluation. Most patients understand this relationship, though some will occasionally try to bring whatever influence they might have to assure that the neuropsychologist is adequately informed.

In more typical clinical settings, neuropsychologists must balance the risks of offending a patient with the reasonable practice of setting firm boundaries. Both approaches are defensible, though the clinician should be prepared to explain their policy in a matter-or-fact way. Some may choose to simply not see patients with clear indications of somatoform symptomatology. However, given the ubiquitous nature of somatization, such practitioners are not likely to be clinically overburdened. Despite the fact that this kind of contact does not occur frequently, management of somatizing patients from the outset of our contact with them is important because it should set a professional and respectful tone for the remainder of the evaluation and subsequent referrals.

Clinical Interview

In most cases, the clinical interview is the neuropsychologist's first encounter with a patient. As such, this represents a critical point in the neuropsychologist–patient relationship. While this may seem overstated, first impressions are very important to patients and likely more so to somatizing patients. The anxiety that patients may have about the assessment process can be either heightened or significantly allayed in the first few minutes of the clinical interview. If a patient perceives the clinician as distant or critical, this is likely to affect most other aspects of the evaluation process. Many patients are conditioned to provide information and wait for pronouncements from doctors. Health care's encouragement of patients to be their own advocates has changed this "old school" way of thinking for many patients. The stoic somatizing patient may fit the old model in a bit more stereotypic fashion, whereas the expressive somatizing patient will often go to the other end of the spectrum. It is not unusual for the expressive patient to attempt to control the interview from the outset. Thus, while it is important to be open and kind, it is equally important to establish some boundaries and rules of engagement, as the following example shows:

Dr. B. was a chiropractor who had been involved in a motor vehicle accident, apparently sustaining a mild traumatic brain injury. She was referred by a chiropractic colleague that was treating her for cervical strain injuries. When I went to the waiting room to call Dr. B. she arose quickly, extended her hand, and said "I'm Dr. B., it's nice to meet you." We walked back to my office, and I invited her to have a seat. Dr. B. pulled out a small notebook and said, "I need to make sure that I hit all these points with you, but the first thing I wanted to talk about was my memory problems." She started to talk about problems that she was encountering in her work with patients and how this was affecting her practice. A minute or two into her recitation, I interrupted and said, "I understand that you have a number of concerns, and I would like to make sure that we attend to all of them. It is important for me to go through the interview in my usual fashion to assure that I don't miss any critical details. When I have gone through my list, I'll ask you to come back to any of your concerns that we were unable to discuss. Does that sound reasonable?" "Oh sure," she responded, "It's just that my meetings with other doctors have been so brief and I wanted to make sure that I didn't miss any of the details that I have in the past." I told Dr. B. that I was appreciative of her thoroughness and made sure that I asked her at the end of my interview whether we had touched upon all of her concerns. She took a minute or two to review and restate some of these issues, and it was clear that we had covered them all. As I escorted Dr. B. to the waiting area, she said, "Thank you Greg, this has been very helpful, I look forward to meeting with you again."

On the other end of the spectrum, stoic patients may be loathe to elaborate on their history, perhaps concerned that it will detract from the issue at hand.

Understanding Somatization

While this kind of information is more likely to issue forth from the expressive patient, it is important for clinicians to make sure that important elements of a patient's history are routinely covered. Many times this will be true if there is a history of treatment for substance abuse or a "nervous breakdown." Somatizing patients are often wary of reporting this kind of information for fear that it will detract from more central issues (in their opinion). Further, it is often the case that patients have been treated following similar incidents or diagnoses in the past. If the neuropsychologist does not inquire specifically about previous head trauma, treatment for various medical/neuropsychiatric diagnoses in the past, or instances of short/long-term disability, these might not be offered by the patient. On occasion, patients will wonder aloud why such "personal" details are relevant. As with the early parts of the clinical interview, the importance of a thorough review of history should be emphasized because this is often an abiding concern for somatizing patients. Whether or not such information is ultimately disclosed by the patient is at their discretion, though it is important to put forth an expectation of earnest and cooperative communication.

In the course of a sometimes lengthy clinical interview, it is important to allow patients to share difficult information and to give them time to recover from a painful disclosure. Somatizing patients will often express a sense of embarrassment in showing their emotions, and this should be dealt with much as it would be in a psychotherapeutic context. They should be reassured that it is acceptable to experience and show emotion when talking about these difficult issues. Of course, unlike the psychotherapy context, there is a need to move forward, and this needs to be accomplished adroitly.

If a patient is intent on commandeering the assessment process, it will most likely occur during the initial interview. This is more likely to happen in forensic contexts when there would appear to be some considerable risk to the patient to going through with an evaluation. That is, if patients with clear secondary gain issues suspect that the evaluation might affect their circumstances negatively, they may come in with a strategy of derailing the evaluation with emotional outbursts and claims that they simply cannot go through with the assessment. This is much less likely to happen in a routine clinical context, though there are often similar circumstances where the somatizing patient might perceive a loss by losing their standing as an impaired patient.

In the most general terms, the neuropsychologist should labor to present as both serious and affable. Many somatizing patients are likely to have encountered prickly clinicians who make little effort to disguise their frustration, disbelief, or even contempt for the patient. This taps into an entrenched dynamic for the patient and will never result in a positive outcome. Doctors who are "mean" or rude to somatizing patients will be reflexively cast in the role of abusers or charlatans, regardless of their credentials or actual ability. While it may seem that there is a fine line between a patient's perceptions of these things and reality, it is probably not as fine as it seems. Again, critical self-examination of one's clinical interactions is something that should be routinely practiced.

Neuropsychological Evaluation

The test administration portion of the neuropsychological evaluation differs depending on whether neuropsychologists administer test measures themselves or use a psychometrist or technician. Neuropsychologists who do their own testing should already have set the foundation for what is to come in the next part of the evaluation process. That is, during the clinical interview, they should be clear about the importance of progressing through measures with a limited amount of conversation about the tests and/or feedback about how the patient is performing. Patients will frequently ask how they performed. They might also express concern or consternation when they feel they have performed poorly. Regardless of whether neuropsychologists administer tests themselves or with the assistance of a psychometrist, patients should be alerted to the fact that there is considerable variability in the nature of the tests that will be administered. I like to emphasize that some measures are quite simple and others quite challenging. I ask them to keep in mind that it is likely that they will feel they have done poorly on some tasks and that this is not necessarily an indication of a serious problem. By preparing patients in this fashion, it is easier to assuage their anxiety about challenging tests. While it is reasonable to expend some effort in calming patients during testing, it is also necessary to keep things moving at a reasonable pace. Instead of spending time talking about what is behind patients' anxiety or emotional reactions, it is probably more practical to recommend a short break for patients to compose themselves.

Recent surveys have indicated that most neuropsychologists employ psychometrists or technicians in their practices (Sweet, Nelson, & Moberg, 2006). Surveys have also indicated that there is some variability in the educational background and training of technicians (Sweet, Peck, Abramowitz, & Etzweiler, 2002; Sweet et al., 2006). As such, it can be expected that some technicians will be adept at dealing with the vagaries of testing somatizing patients, while others might struggle considerably. The responsibility for preparing psychometrists to deal with difficult patients obviously rests with the neuropsychologist. I do not believe that depth of educational background necessarily prepares a psychometrist to deal effectively with difficult patients. Some will feel comfortable, and some considerably anxious. Regardless, technicians should be empowered to be firm and expeditious in their approach to completing tests. This will be facilitated by neuropsychologists' affirmation of their psychometrists' expertise and experience when discussing upcoming testing during the clinical interview. Patient should be made aware that their questions about tests and their performance will need to be deferred until a feedback session is conducted with the neuropsychologist.

Mr. P. was a 52-year-old man with chronic low back pain and recent onset of memory/cognitive concerns following a four-vessel coronary artery bypass grafting. In addition to these concerns, the patient had been on Social Security disability for more than 10 years secondary to depression, anxiety, and "severe veritable [sic] bowel disease." Mr. P. was interviewed for approximately one hour and was administered a couple of brief tests in the neuropsychologist's office. He was given a 15-minute break, and testing was resumed by a psychometrist. Mr. P. immediately commented on the use of the psychometrist and asked a number of questions about her educational background and number of years of experience. He seemed affable at first, but it quickly became clear that he was agitated when given tests that required him to perform as quickly as possible. He protested the relevance of the tests, saying that he was having problems with memory and "not this kind of silly BS." Despite the psychometrist's encouragement and reassurance that he was performing adequately, Mr. P. began to complain of severe back pain and stiffness. He was offered a brief break, but declined. The psychometrist encouraged him to take a break because she needed to consult with the neuropsychologist. He decided to take a short break. The neuropsychologist returned to speak with the patient and asked if there was anything that could be done to make him more comfortable. Mr. P. said that he was "just fine" and felt that he was doing well on tests. When the psychometrist returned to resume testing, the patient was sullen and abrupt but did not put up any further obstacles to collecting the test data.

In extreme situations, a patient's recalcitrance during testing can be cause for terminating the exam. In my experience, this most often happens in the medicolegal context. The neuropsychologist needs to give serious consideration to a range of threats to validity based on these kinds of behaviors. Even when patients pass some symptom validity measures, their distractibility and hostility must be considered possible threats to obtaining adequate assessment data. Chapter 5 discusses a number of psychometric measures that can effectively be utilized in determining the validity of patients' responses. However, intratest behaviors remain important as ecologically valid indications of performance validity. Such behaviors speak volumes to our non-neuropsychologist colleagues, as well as to individuals outside of the health care context, such as judges and juries.

The Evaluation Report

In many cases, the only opportunity neuropsychologists have to convey their evaluation results is in the form of a narrative report. While this does not involve direct contact with the patient, it is reasonable and prudent to assume that the patient will be reviewing the report. Further, the narrative report is the enduring documentation of the evaluation process. There are many places to misstep in the crafting of an evaluation report, and many different views of what constitutes an adequate or good report. My comments here focus mainly on narrative content in the context of a report describing patients with significant somatoform symptomatology. The more general topic of report writing in neuropsychology is addressed by other sources (Donders, 2001a, 2001b; Wong, 2006) and is not discussed at length in this brief section.

In their narrative reports on somatizing patients, neuropsychologists routinely use such terms as "somatization" and "conversion" and explain symptoms as "out of proportion to objective findings." These descriptors are often factually accurate but can be offensive and inscrutable to patients. Other words such as unrealistic, exaggerated, and hysterical convey information to other professionals that might be useful, though to the patient these can be perceived as pejorative and minimizing. Importantly in this context, such terminology might also keep the patient from hearing a more essential message regarding treatment recommendations. There is a fine line between conveying results in an accurate and dispassionate manner and writing in a way that will belittle or embarrass a struggling patient. A related issue is the not so subtle tipping of one's hand to other clinicians. One need not look far to find associates that have a misanthropic view of somatizing patients. There is no need to reinforce these views with a written version of a wink and nudge. Sharing biases in this manner will only assure that these patients will be regarded warily and perhaps even with hostility by those who encounter them in the future. Our use of verbal and written language is crucial, and ironically, some neuropsychologists seem not to appreciate (or simply to ignore) these nuances. Below I have excerpted two examples from the impressions section of a neuropsychological evaluation report, which contrast different styles of reporting essentially the same results:

> Mr. X. complains of an exceedingly large number of somatoform symptoms. These include muscle soreness, weakness, and pain in the neck and shoulders that the patient says are associated with his fibromyalgia. There are also many vague symptoms such as headaches, upset stomach, dizziness, blurred vision, impotence, generalized joint pain, paresthesias, and severe low back pain. None of the symptoms appears to be related to a diagnosis offered by a qualified specialist or a known disease process. Mr. X. shows extreme elevations on MMPI-2 scales measuring subjective distress. This calls into question the validity of his responses on a number of other self-report measures. Despite the questionable validity due to reporting of distress, the patient shows a typical somatization or conversion profile with a high level of vague symptom report and poor psychological insight. This combination typically results in increased physical symptom reporting under stressful circumstances. It seems clear, given the patient's essentially normal neuropsychological profile, that the symptoms are psychologically based and not related to actual pathology.

In contrast, a very similar case was reported in the following manner, avoiding some pejorative references and a strong suggestion that there is nothing "organically" wrong with the patient:

Ms. A. reports a very high level of physical discomfort across a number of different bodily systems. There are reports of frequent headaches, stomach and GI disturbances, low back pain, fatigue, concentration difficulties, forgetfulness, and general malaise. In addition, the patient acknowledges very high levels of depression and anxiety symptomatology on standardized measures and during the clinical interview. Despite these concerns, Ms. A. shows no normative neuropsychological deficits across a wide range of cognitive domains. As such, Ms. A.'s various symptoms do not appear to relate to a singular cause. Further, the patient is likely to experience an increase in symptoms when under a high level of psychological stress. In Ms. A.'s case there has been increased stress due to the loss of her job and a pending divorce. It is clear that the relationship between the patient's health concerns, reported cognitive difficulties, and significant current stressors is complex and very disruptive for her at the present time.

The first report excerpt states with certainty that the reported symptoms and deficits are likely psychological, while the second excerpt is more circumspect in attributing the etiology to a specific or singular cause. Interestingly, the description of somatoform symptoms in the first report is very much consistent with the *DSM* typology against which many have railed. Underlying the first report is the belief that psychological and biological causes of discomfort are separable. By contrast, the second report conveys an appreciation of the complexity of the symptoms and of the interaction between a person and his or her environment.

The stylistic choices highlighted above are not unusual. The first example uses definitive language and provides a clear characterization of the neuropsychologist's diagnostic formulation. Such language is often used in reports generated for medicolegal purposes and thus are by definition based on a binary view of the world. There is typically a clear directive to be definitive and pointed. The purpose of such of report is quite different from the clinical context from which the second excerpt may have originated. A forensic report seeks to assist the trier of fact, whereas a clinical report seeks to assist the referring clinician. Debates about the accuracy or correctness of such approaches are beyond the scope of this brief discussion. However, somatizing patients do seem to polarize neuropsychologists' views of the purpose of a consultation report (as well as many other aspects of the evaluation enterprise).

Feedback Sessions

A common element of the neuropsychological evaluation process is providing feedback regarding the assessment results. It is not always the case that patients want to meet to review the evaluation results, though they often do. In my practice setting with a large neurology group, patients will typically first meet with the referring neurologist to review my evaluation and any other studies that have been ordered. I encourage patients to schedule a feedback session with me if they are interested in going over the results in more detail and/or receiving a copy of my consultation report. Once again, there is variability in how feedback is provided. In rare instances, such as hospital consultation services, patients may be given some manner of feedback on the same day as their assessment. More typically, feedback sessions are scheduled a week to several weeks out from the initial assessment date.

I have found feedback sessions to be less predictable in terms of typical responses of a somatizing patient. Reactions have ranged from preferring not to meet for a feedback session at all, to hostile confrontation regarding the findings of my evaluation. In my experience, it is difficult to impress upon patients the importance of a thorough review of the assessment if they are disinclined to do this. For some patients, there may be a sense that the evaluation was not particularly availing or helpful. In other words, the evaluation is not likely to provide them with answers they want to hear. Such patients are unlikely to schedule follow-up appointments or, if they do, will not make the appointments. They may have the feeling that they have heard it all before and do not want to contend with in other health care provider giving them "bad news." While I have felt that it would be worthwhile to go over test results with such patients, the effort is typically not very productive and often results in gaps in one's schedule.

A subset of somatizing patients makes an earnest effort to come in to review the results of the evaluation. They are reasonably open to hearing about the results and express a sense of understanding of the findings. In the course of providing feedback to such a patient, it is tempting to believe that some progress is being made. Patients will shake their head in understanding and will generally be agreeable while they are receiving information. Much of the time, the depth of this understanding is betrayed when the patient acknowledges the feedback but counters with a "yes, but" response:

Ms. H. was a 32-year-old female who was seen for evaluation secondary to memory and concentration problems following an accident at work when she was struck on the head by a box of copier paper that fell from a storage shelf. Ms. H. put forth a strong effort and performed well on most measures administered in the neuropsychological evaluation. Her MMPI-2 profile was prototypical for somatization, and she showed mild to moderate depression and anxiety symptomatology, as well as significant distress and feelings of alienation. Throughout my description an explanation of her concerns, the patient was attentive and frequently shook her head in agreement, even when I described the dynamics of conversion and somatoform symptoms. When I finished speaking, the patient responded, "Yes, I can see how that would all work. I think I would like to give the psychotherapy a chance, but I would first like to just find a way, like a medication or something, that would help me focus better. When I can figure out what's wrong with my brain and get it back to normal, then I think I'll be ready to talk with a therapist."

Not all patients resist the interpretation of results that suggest somatization and little in the way of neuropsychological deficits. Some genuinely struggle with their symptoms, the complexity of their situation, and the fact that psychological factors play a very significant role in their discomfort. Of course, these are the patients that are most likely to benefit from referral for psychotherapy and other management approaches. On the far end of the spectrum are the expressive patients who know what the outcome of the assessment should be and resist any other outcome as an indication of the practitioner's incompetence or lack of knowledge. Such patients may come back to review exam results and will engage in debates about the merits of the evaluation findings. While such patients should be thoroughly briefed, there is not typically much benefit to engaging beyond the conveyance of results and a brief restatement of recommendations.

Referral for Services

Among all of the topics discussed in this chapter, referring patients for services is probably the area in which there is most disparity. In urban centers or communities with university-based training programs, there are likely a large number of different resources for patients with somatoform symptoms. In contrast, smaller or more rural communities may have very limited mental health resources in general, let alone more specific resources for somatizing patients. Therefore, it is critical that neuropsychologists educate themselves regarding the talents of their therapist colleagues. Consultation with colleagues and a wide range of other health care providers is not typically an empirical or data-based process. Aside from basic knowledge of the therapeutic techniques used by a therapist, referrers are often left to their decidedly unscientific devices to determine who constitutes good therapists for their patients. Most often, such information comes from recommendations from colleagues or from patients themselves. While it would be helpful to know that a therapist follows a specific program such as that detailed by Woolfolk and Allen (2007), most of the time this can be determined only through direct contact and lengthy discussion with a therapist. My practice setting is located in a metropolitan area where there are several hundred licensed psychologists and manifold other therapists and counselors. To compile a comprehensive list of qualified therapists would be a massive and unwieldy undertaking. Therefore, most of us are left to choose from a handful of colleagues and programs that we judge to be competent based on our sense of their abilities, colleagues' recommendations, and comments from patients who have had experiences with them.

As mentioned in chapter 6, most neuropsychologists do not conduct individual psychotherapy, though most have a need to refer patients for mental health services. Neuropsychologists typically see their primary role as providing quality diagnostic services, but they also routinely provide consultation and referral services. The services for which patients are recommended will naturally follow biases held by the neuropsychologist. For instance, it is fairly common for patients evaluated by neuropsychologists to have mood and anxiety symptoms. As such, referral for treatment, usually pharmacologic, is common. Depending upon the setting, some neuropsychologists will be pressed to make recommendations for pharmacological treatment. Minimally, directing patients toward appropriate resources such as psychiatrists or geriatricians will be expected. Further, other neurodiagnostic services such as electrographic studies, neuroimaging, or a neurological exam are also frequently recommended.

Chapter 6 discusses the range of primarily psychological treatments with which neuropsychologists should be familiar. So, armed with a solid knowledge of the psychological treatment literature and having an array of treatment services at one's disposal, neuropsychologists should be able to make referrals that will help their somatizing patients. This all seems straightforward enough, but in order for patients to benefit from a knowledgeable referral, they need to feel like a respectful and professional relationship was forged with their neuropsychologist. It will matter little whether the evaluation was expertly executed and reported if the patient was offended or otherwise put off by the neuropsychologist. In addition, the quality of a therapist or program will not matter if a reasonable relationship has not been established. This is ultimately the reason that understanding somatizing patients more completely is so important. It might also be a primary difference between forensic assessment and routine clinical referrals. The former will not typically involve specific treatment recommendations, while the purpose of the latter is to do just that. Aside from the nuts and bolts of neuropsychological assessment, clinical acumen and sensitivity will always play a crucial role in this process. Of course, this is not only true for somatizing patients, though they do represent a particularly challenging end of the spectrum.

As "treating neuropsychologists," most of us have an interest in providing the patient and our referral source with something useful. Clear explanations of neuropsychological test data are not always what our customers need most. For many referral sources, there is an expectation that the neuropsychologist will provide not only a solid technical assessment but also feedback regarding how a patient can best be served. Given the foregoing, is very important that we be able to have our recommendations followed. First, it seems that this is more likely when the quality of the relationship established between the neuropsychologist and the patient is solid, respectful, and supportive. Second, if patients are adequately educated about the nature and complexity of their situation/diagnosis, they are more likely to understand the importance of a wide-ranging treatment approach involving psychotherapy and other psychologically oriented interventions. Finally, patients should be referred to a knowledgeable professional and/or program that will also treat them with respect and convey a strong sense of hope that progress can be made.

Conclusion

Too often, we minimize or denigrate the plight of patients that would seem to be wasting our time. We may not take the time to reflect on what it is that bothers us about these patients and may simply act out by "giving them what they deserve." Simply being courteous is not a panacea, but somatizing patients often encounter treating personnel, from top to bottom, who are dismissive or disrespectful. These encounters often harden patients' resolve in terms of finding a "respectable" illness or disorder. Their indignation at being considered mentally ill or weak may seem part and parcel of their problems, but it may also be a reflection of a much larger societal problem.

I close with the notion that somatoform disorders seem to be of greatest concern in cultures and countries that value hard work and fear or loathe personal weakness. Indeed, the dynamic described in abusive families where there is a tyranny of high expectations and severe punishment for lapses is not unlike a larger societal dynamic that punishes or demeans a person's limitations and unrealistically celebrates concrete successes. Ironically, somatizing patients are most rigid and intolerant of people and behaviors that closely mirror their own. As treating clinicians, we have the opportunity to model a more tolerant and understanding approach to dealing with interpersonal limitations. If we falter in this regard, the prospects for moving patients toward a better understanding of their issues and encouraging them to seek appropriate interventions will be limited, and an unfortunately familiar cycle will persist.

References

American Board of Psychiatry and Neurology. (2008). http://www.abpn.com/ spec_subspec_description.htm#psychmed. Retrieved August 2008.

Ainsworth, M. D. S. (1967). *Infancy in Uganda: Infant Care and the Growth of Love.* Baltimore, MD: Johns Hopkins University Press.

Aklin, W. M., & Turner, S. M. (2006). Toward understanding ethnic and cultural factors in the interviewing process. *Psychotherapy: Theory, Research, Practice, Training, 43,* 50–64.

Alexander, M. P. (1992). Neuropsychiatric correlates of persistent postconcussive syndrome. *Journal of Head Trauma Rehabilitation, 7,* 60–69.

Allen, L. A., Escobar, J. I., Lehrer, P. M., Gara, M. A., & Woolfolk, R. L. (2002). Psychosocial treatments for multiple unexplained physical symptoms: A review of the literature. *Psychosomatic Medicine, 64,* 939–950.

Allen, L. A., Woolfolk, R. L., Escobar, J. I., Gara, M. A., & Hamer, R. M. (2006). Cognitive-behavioral therapy for somatization disorder: A randomized controlled trial. *Archives of Internal Medicine, 166,* 1512–1518.

Allen, L. A., Woolfolk, R. L., Lehrer, P. M., Gara, M. A., & Escobar, J. I. (2001). Cognitive behavior therapy for somatization disorder: A preliminary investigation. *Journal of Behavior Therapy and Experimental Psychiatry, 32,* 53–62.

American Psychiatric Association. (1968). *Diagnostic and Statistical Manual of Mental Disorders,* 2nd ed. Washington, DC: Author.

American Psychiatric Association. (1980). *Diagnostic and Statistical Manual of Mental Disorders,* 3rd ed. Washington, DC: Author.

American Psychiatric Association. (1987). *Diagnostic and Statistical Manual of Mental Disorders,* 3rd ed. revised. Washington, DC: Author.

American Psychiatric Association. (1994). *Diagnostic and Statistical Manual of Mental Disorders,* 4th ed. Washington, DC: Author.

Arbisi, P. A., & Butcher, J. N. (2004). Failure of the FBS to predict malingering of somatic symptoms: Response to critiques by Greve and

Bianchini and Lees-Haley and Fox. *Archives of Clinical Neuropsychology, 19,* 341–345.

Ardila, A., Rosselli, M., & Puente, A. E. (1994). *Neuropsychological Evaluation of the Spanish speaker.* New York: Plenum Press.

Arnow, B. A., Hunkeler, E. M., Blasey, C. M., Lee, J., Constantino, M. J., Fireman, B., et al. (2006). Comorbid depression, chronic pain, and disability in primary care. *Psychosomatic Medicine, 68,* 262–268.

Artiola i Fortuny, L., & Mullaney, H. (1998). Assessing patients whose language you do not know: Can the absurd be ethical? *Clinical Neuropsychologist, 12,* 113–126.

Barsky, A. J., & Borus, J. F. (1999). Functional somatic syndromes. *Annals of Internal Medicine, 130,* 910–921.

Barsky, A. J., Orav, E. J., & Bates, D. W. (2005). Somatization increases medical utilization and costs independent of psychiatric and medical comorbidity. *Archives of General Psychiatry, 62,* 903–910.

Barsky, A. J., & Wyshak, G. (1990). Hypochondriasis and somatosensory amplification. *British Journal of Psychiatry, 157,* 404–409.

Bartholomew, K., & Horowitz, L. M. (1991). Attachment styles among young adults: A test of a four-category model. *Journal of Personality & Social Psychology, 61,* 226–244.

Benedict R. H. B., Munschauer, F., Linn, R., Miller, C., Murphy, E., Foley, F., Jacobs, L. (2003). Screening for MS Cognitive Impairment using a Self-Administered 15-Item Questionnaire. *Multiple Sclerosis, 9,* 95–101.

Benedict, R. H. B., Cookfair, D., Gavett, R., Gunther, M., Munschauer, F., & Garg, N., et al. (2006). Validity of the minimal assessment of cognitive function in multiple sclerosis (MACFIMS). *Journal of the International Neuropsychological Society, 12,* 549–558.

Ben-Porath, Y. S., & Tellegen, A. (2006). *MMPI-2 Fake Bad Scale (FBS).* Retrieved from University of Minnesota Press Web site: www.upress.umn.edu/tests/mmpi2_fbs.html. Retrieved August 2008.

Bianchini, K. J., Greve, K. W., & Glynn, G. (2005). On the diagnosis of malingered pain-related disability: Lessons from cognitive malingering research. *Spine Journal, 5,* 404–417.

Bigler, E. D. (2003). Neurobiology and neuropathology underlie the neuropsychological deficits associated with traumatic brain injury. *Archives of Clinical Neuropsychology, 18,* 595–621.

Binder, L. M. (2005). Forensic assessment of medically unexplained symptoms. In G. J. Larrabee (Ed.), *Forensic Neuropsychology: A Scientific Approach*. New York: Oxford University Press.

Binder, L. M., & Campbell, K. A. (2004). Medically unexplained symptoms and neuropsychological assessment. *Journal of Clinical and Experimental Neuropsychology, 26*, 369–392.

Binder, L. M., Kindermann, S. S., Heaton, R. K., & Salinsky, M. C. (1998). Neuropsychologic impairment in patients with nonepileptic seizures. *Archives of Clinical Neuropsychology, 13*, 513–522.

Binder, L. M., Rohling, M. L., & Larrabee, G. J. (1997). A review of mild head trauma. Part I: Meta analytic review of neuropsychological studies. *Journal of Clinical and Experimental Neuropsychology, 19*, 421–431.

Binder, L. M., Salinsky, M. C., & Smith, S. P. (1994). Psychological correlates of psychogenic seizures. *Journal of Clinical and Experimental Neuropsychology, 16*, 524–530.

Binder, L. M., Storzbach, D., & Salinsky, M. C. (2006). MMPI-2 profiles of persons with multiple chemical sensitivity. *Clinical Neuropsychologist, 20*, 848–857.

Bobholz, J. H., & Rao, S. M. (2003). Cognitive dysfunction in multiple sclerosis: A review of recent developments. *Current Opinion in Neurology, 16*, 283–288.

Bowlby, J. (1969), *Attachment and Loss*, Vol. 1: *Attachment*. New York: Basic Books.

Bowlby, J. (1973). *Attachment and Loss*, Vol. 2: *Separation*. New York: Basic Books.

Boyce, P. M., Talley, N. J., Balaam, B., Koloski, N. A., & Truman, G. (2003). A randomized controlled trial of cognitive behavior therapy, relaxation training, and routine clinical care for the irritable bowel syndrome. *American Journal of Gastroenterology, 98*, 2209–2218.

Brands, A. M., Kessels, R. P., Hoogma, R. P., Henselmans, J. M., van der Beek Boter, J. W., Kappelle, L. J., et al. (2006). Cognitive performance, psychological well-being, and brain magnetic resonance imaging in older patients with type 1 diabetes. *Diabetes, 55*, 1800–1806.

Brands, A. M., van den Berg, E., Manschot, S. M., Biessels, G. J., Kappelle, L. J., de Haan, E. H., et al. (2007). A detailed profile of cognitive dysfunction and its relation to psychological distress in patients with type 2 diabetes mellitus. *Journal of the International Neuropsychological Society, 13,* 288–297.

Breuer, J., Freud, S., & Strachey, J. (trans.) (1957). *Studies on Hysteria.* New York: Basic Books.

Briquet, P. (1859). *Traité Clinique et Thérapeutique de l'Hysterie.* Paris: Bailliere.

Brown, M. C., Levin, B. E., Ramsay, R. E., & Katz, D. A. (1991). Characteristics of patients with nonepileptic seizures. *Journal of Epilepsy, 4*(4), 225–229.

Brown, R. J. (2004). Psychological mechanisms of medically unexplained symptoms: An integrative conceptual model. *Psychological Bulletin, 130,* 793–812.

Brown, R. J., Schrag, A., & Trimble, M. R. (2005). Dissociation, childhood interpersonal trauma, and family functioning in patients with somatization disorder. *American Journal of Psychiatry, 162,* 899–905.

Bruck, W., & Stadelmann, C. (2005). The spectrum of multiple sclerosis: New lessons from pathology. *Current Opinions in Neurology, 18,* 221–224.

Busichio, K., Tiersky, L. A., DeLuca, J., & Natelson, B. H. (2004). Neuropsychological deficits in patients with chronic fatigue syndrome. *Journal of the International Neuropsychological Society, 10,* 278–285.

Buss, D. M. (1999). *Evolutionary Psychology. The New Science of the Mind.* New York: Allyn & Bacon.

Butcher, J. N., Arbisi, P. A., Atlis, M. M., & McNulty, J. L. (2003). The construct validity of the Lees-Haley Fake Bad Scale. Does this scale measure somatic malingering and feigned emotional distress? *Archives of Clinical Neuropsychology, 18,* 473–485.

Butcher, J. N., Dahlstrom, W. G., Graham, J. R., Tellegen, A., & Kaemmer, B. (1989). *Manual for Administration and Scoring of the MMPI-2.* Minneapolis: University of Minnesota Press.

Campo, J. V., & Fritz, G. (2001). A management model for pediatric somatization. *Psychosomatics, 42,* 467–476.

Campo, J. V., Jansen-McWilliams, L., Comer, D. M., & Kelleher, K. J. (1999). Somatization in pediatric primary care: Association with psychopathology, functional impairment, and use of services. *Journal of the American Academy of Child and Adolescent Psychiatry, 38,* 1093–1101.

Carson, A. J., Best, S., Postma, K., Stone, J., Warlow, C., & Sharpe, M. (2003). The outcome of neurology outpatients with medically unexplained symptoms: A prospective cohort study. *Journal of Neurology Neurosurgery and Psychiatry, 74,* 897–900.

Carson, A. J., Ringbauer, B., Stone, J., McKenzie, L., Warlow, C., & Sharpe, M. (2000). Do medically unexplained symptoms matter? A prospective cohort study of 300 new referrals to neurology outpatient clinics. *Journal of Neurology Neurosurgery and Psychiatry, 68,* 207–210.

Castellon, S. A., Ganz, P. A., Bower, J. E., Petersen, L., Abraham, L., & Greendale, G. A. (2004). Neurocognitive performance in breast cancer survivors exposed to adjuvant chemotherapy and tamoxifen. *Journal of Clinical and Experimental Neuropsychology, 26,* 955–969.

Carone, D. A., Benedict, R. H., Munschauer, F. E., 3rd, Fishman, I., & Weinstock-Guttman, B. (2005). Interpreting patient/informant discrepancies of reported cognitive symptoms in MS. *Journal of the International Neuropsychological Society, 11,* 574–583.

Christodoulou, C., Deluca, J., Johnson, S. K., Lange, G., Gaudino, E. A., & Natelson, B. H. (1999). Examination of Cloninger's basic dimensions of personality in fatiguing illness: Chronic fatigue syndrome and multiple sclerosis. *Journal of Psychosomatic Research, 47,* 597–607.

Ciechanowski, P. S., Walker, E. A., Katon, W. J., & Russo, J. E. (2002). Attachment theory: A model for health care utilization and somatization. *Psychosomatic Medicine, 64,* 660–667.

Cloninger, C. R., Martin, R. L., Guze, S. B., & Clayton, P. J. (1986). A prospective follow-up and family study of somatization in men and women. *American Journal of Psychiatry, 143,* 873–878.

Collins, M. W., Grindel, S. H., Lovell, M. R., Dede, D. E., Moser, D. J., Phalin, B. R., Nogle, S., Wasik, M., Cordry, D., Daugherty, M. K., Sears, S. F., Nicolette, G., Indelicato, P., & McKeag, D. B. (1999). Relationship Between Concussion and Neuropsychological Performance in College Football Players. *JAMA, 282,* 964–970.

Cote, K. A., & Moldofsky, H. (1997). Sleep, daytime symptoms, and cognitive performance in patients with fibromyalgia. *Journal of Rheumatology, 24,* 2014–2023.

Cragar, D. E., Berry, D. T. R., Fakhoury, T. A., Cibula, J. E., & Schmitt, F. A. (2006). Performance of patients with epilepsy or psychogenic nonepileptic seizures on four measures of effort. *Clinical Neuropsychologist, 20,* 552–566.

Creed, F., Fernandes, L., Guthrie, E., Palmer, S., Ratcliffe, J., Read, N., et al. (2003). The cost-effectiveness of psychotherapy and paroxetine for severe irritable bowel syndrome. *Gastroenterology, 124,* 303–317.

Creed, F., Guthrie, E., Ratcliffe, J., Fernandes, L., Rigby, C., Tomenson, B., et al. (2005). Reported sexual abuse predicts impaired functioning but a good response to psychological treatments in patients with severe irritable bowel syndrome. *Psychosomatic Medicine, 67,* 490–499.

Cull, A., Hay, C., Love, S. B., Mackie, M., Smets, E., & Stewart, M. (1996).What do patients mean when they complain of concentration and memory problems? *British Journal of Cancer, 74,* 1674–1679.

Daly, E., Komaroff, A. L., Bloomingdale, K., Wilson, S., & Albert, M. S. (2001). Neuropsychological function in patients with chronic fatigue syndrome, multiple sclerosis, and depression. *Applied Neuropsychology, 8,* 12–22.

Damasio, A. (1994). *Descartes' Error: Emotion, Reason, and the Human Brain.* New York: Penguin Books.

Dana, R. H. (1996). Culturally competent assessment practice in the United States. *Journal of Personality Assessment, 66,* 472–487.

Davanloo, H. (1995). *Unlocking the Unconscious: Selected Papers of Habib Davanloo.* Oxford: John Wiley & Sons.

Deale, A., Husain, K., Chalder, T., & Wessely, S. (2001). Long-term outcome of cognitive behavior therapy versus relaxation therapy for chronic fatigue syndrome: A 5-year follow-up study. *American Journal of Psychiatry, 158,* 2038–2042.

DeLuca, J., Johnson, S. K., Beldowicz, D., & Natelson, B. H. (1995). Neuropsychological impairments in chronic fatigue syndrome, multiple sclerosis, and depression. *Journal of Neurology, Neurosurgery & Psychiatry, 58,* 38–43.

DeLuca, J., Johnson, S. K., & Natelson, B. H. (1993). Information processing efficiency in chronic fatigue syndrome and multiple sclerosis. *Archives of Neurology, 50,* 301–304.

Dendy, C., Cooper, M., & Sharpe, M. (2001). Interpretation of symptoms in chronic fatigue syndrome. *Behaviour Research and Therapy, 39,* 1369–1380.

Derogatis, L. R. (1992). SCL-90-R: *Administration, scoring and procedure manual—II*. Baltimore, MD: Clinical Psychometric Research.

Dewhurst, K. (1966). *Dr. Thomas Sydenham (1624–1689): His Life and Original Writings*. Berkeley: University of California Press.

Dikmen, S. S., Machamer, J. E., Winn, H. R., & Temkin, N. R. (1995). Neuropsychological outcome at 1-year post head injury. *Neuropsychology, 9*, 80–90. Donders, J. (2001a). A survey of report writing by neuropsychologists, I: General characteristics and content. *Clinical Neuropsychologist, 15*, 137–149.

Donders, J. (2001b). A survey of report writing by neuropsychologists, II: Test data, report format, and document length. *Clinical Neuropsychologist, 15*, 150–161.

Drane, D. L., Williamson, D. J., Stroup, E. S., Holmes, M. D., Jung, M., Koerner, E., et al. (2006). Cognitive impairment is not equal in patients with epileptic and psychogenic nonepileptic seizures. *Epilepsia, 47*(11), 1879–1886.

Drossman, D. A., Toner, B. B., Whitehead, W. E., Diamant, N. E., Dalton, C. B., Duncan, S., et al. (2003). Cognitive-behavioral therapy versus education and desipramine versus placebo for moderate to severe functional bowel disorders. *Gastroenterology, 125*, 19–31.

Engel, C. C. (2006). Explanatory and pragmatic perspectives regarding idiopathic physical symptoms and related syndromes. *CNS Spectrums, 11*, 225–232.

Escobar, J. I., Burnam, M. A., Karno, M., Forsythe, A., & Golding, J. M. (1987). Somatization in the community. *Archives of General Psychiatry, 44*, 713–718.

Escobar, J. I., Waitzkin, H., Silver, R. C., Gara, M., & Holman, A. (1998). Abridged somatization: A study in primary care. *Psychosomatic Medicine, 60*, 466–472.

Feighner, J. P., Robins, E., Guze, S. B., Woodruff, R. A., Winokur, G., & Munoz, R. (1972). Diagnostic criteria for use in psychiatric research. *Archives of General Psychiatry, 26*, 57–63.

Fenichel, O. (1945). *The Psychoanalytic Theory of Neurosis*. New York: W. W. Norton.

Fiedler, N., Kipen, H. M., DeLuca, J., & Kelly-McNeil, K. (1996). A controlled comparison of multiple chemical sensitivities and chronic fatigue syndrome. *Psychosomatic Medicine, 58*, 38–49.

Fiedler, N., Kipen, H., Deluca, J., Kelly-McNeil, K., & Natelson, B. (1994). Neuropsychology and psychology of MCS. *Toxicology and Industrial Health, 10*, 545–554.

Fink, P., Hansen, M. S., & Sondergaard, L. (2005). Somatoform disorders among first-time referrals to a neurology service. *Psychosomatics, 46*, 540–548.

Fordyce, W. E. (1976). *Behavioral Methods for Chronic Pain and Illness.* St. Louis, MO: Mosby.

Fordyce, W. E., Fowler, R. S., Lehmann, J. R., DeLateur, B. J., Sand, P. L., & Trieschmann, R. B. (1973). Operant conditioning in the treatment of chronic pain. *Archives of Physical Medicine and Rehabilitation, 54*, 399–408.

Fox, D. D., Lees-Haley, P. R., Earnest, K., & Dolezal-Wood, S. (1995). Base rates of post-concussive symptoms in health maintenance organization patients and controls. *Neuropsychology, 9*, 606–611.

Frencham, K. A. R., Fox, A. M., & Maybery, M. T. (2005). Neuropsychological studies of mild traumatic brain injury: A meta-analytic review of research since 1995. *Journal of Clinical and Experimental Neuropsychology, 27*, 334–351.

Frith, C. D., & Frith, U. (2006). How we predict what other people are going to do? *Brain Research, 1079*, 36–46.

Fritz, G. K., Fritsch, S., & Hagino, O. (1997). Somatoform disorders in children and adolescents: A review of the past 10 years. *Journal of the American Academy of Child and Adolescent Psychiatry, 36*, 1329–1338.

Gervais, R. (2005, April). *Development of an Empirically Derived Response Bias Scale for the MMPI-2.* Paper presented at the annual MMPI-2 Symposium and Workshops, Ft. Lauderdale, FL.

Gervais, R. O., Ben-Porath, Y. S., Wygant, D. B., & Green, P. (2007). Development and validation of a response bias scale (RBS) for the MMPI-2. *Assessment, 14*, 196–208.

Gervais, R. O., Green, P., Allen, L. M., & Iverson, G. L. (2002). Effects of coaching on symptom validity testing in chronic pain patients presenting for disability assessments. *Journal of Forensic Psychology, 2*, 1–19.

Glass, J. M., Park, D. C., Minear, M., & Crofford, L. J. (2005). Memory beliefs and function in fibromyalgia patients. *Journal of Psychosomatic Research, 58,* 263–269.

González, C. A., & Griffith, E. E. H. (1996). Culture and the diagnosis of somatoform and dissociative disorders. In H. Fabrega, J. Mezzich & A. Kleinman (Eds.), *Culture and Psychiatric Diagnosis: A DSM-IV Perspective.* Washington, DC: American Psychiatric Press.

Gouvier, W. D., Cubic, B., Jones, G., Brantley, P., & Cutlip, Q. (1992). Postconcussion symptoms and daily stress in normal and head injured college populations. *Archives of Clinical Neuropsychology, 7,* 193–211.

Gouvier, W. D., Uddo-Crane, M., & Brown, L. M. (1988). Base rates of post-concussional symptoms. *Archives of Clinical Neuropsychology, 3,* 273–278.

Grace, G. M., Nielson, W. R., Hopkins, M., & Berg, M. A. (1999). Concentration and memory deficits in patients with fibromyalgia syndrome. *Journal of Clinical and Experimental Neuropsychology, 21,* 477–487.

Graham, J. R. (2006). *MMPI-2: Assessing Personality and Psychopathology,* 4th ed. New York: Oxford University Press.

Green, P. (2003). *Green's Word Memory Test. User's Manual.* Edmonton, Canada: Green's Publishing.

Green, P., Allen, L. M., & Astner, K. (1996). *The Word Memory Test: A User's Guide to the Oral and Computer-Administered Forms,* U.S. version 1.1. Durham, NC: Cognisyst.

Greiffenstein, M. F., & Baker, W. J. (2006). Miller was (mostly) right: Head injury severity inversely related to simulation. *Legal and Criminological Psychology, 11,* 131–145.

Greiffenstein, M. F., Baker, W. J., Axelrod, B., Peck, E. A., & Gervais, R. (2004). The Fake Bad Scale and MMPI-2 Family in detection of implausible psychological trauma claims. *Clinical Neuropsychologist, 18,* 573–590.

Greiffenstein, M. F., Baker, W. J., & Gola, T. (1994). Validation of malingered amnesia measures with a large clinical sample. *Psychological Assessment, 6,* 218–224.

Greiffenstein, M. F., Baker, W. J., Gola, T., Donders, J., & Miller, L. (2002). The Fake Bad Scale in atypical and severe closed head injury litigants. *Journal of Clinical Psychology, 58,* 1591–1600.

Greiffenstein, M. F., Fox, D., & Lees-Haley, P. R. (2007). The Fake Bad Scale in the detection of noncredible brain injury claims. In K. Boone (Ed.), *Feigned Neuropsychological Performance* (pp. 270–291). New York: Guilford Press.

Gureje, O., & Simon, G. E. (1999). The natural history of somatization in primary care. *Psychological medicine, 29*, 669–676.

Gureje, O., Simon, G. E., Ustun, T. B., & Goldberg, D. P. (1997). Somatization in cross-cultural perspective: A World Health Organization study in primary care. *American Journal of Psychiatry, 154*, 989–995.

Guthrie, E., Creed, F., Dawson, D., & Tomenson, B. (1991). A controlled trial of psychological treatment for the irritable bowel syndrome. *Gastroenterology, 100*, 450–457.

Guze, S. B. (1993). Genetics of Briquet's syndrome and somatization disorder: A review of family, adoption, and twin studies. *Annals of Clinical Psychiatry, 5*, 225–230.

Harpending, H. C., & Sobus, J. (1987). Sociopathy as an adaptation. *Ethology & Sociobiology, 8*, 63–72.

Hart, R. P., Martelli, M. F., & Zasler, N. D. (2000). Chronic pain and neuropsychological functioning. *Neuropsychology Review, 10*, 131–149.

Hathaway, S. R., & McKinley, J. C. (1943). *The Minnesota Multiphasic Personality Inventory*, rev. ed. (2nd printing). Minneapolis, MN: University of Minnesota.

Henry, G. K., Heilbronner, R. L., Mittenberg, W., & Enders, C. (2006). The Henry-Heilbronner index: A 15-item empirically derived MMPI-2 subscale for identifying probable malingering in personal injury litigants and disability claimants. *Clinical Neuropsychologist, 20*, 786–797.

Hiller, W., Fichter, M. M., & Rief, W. (2003). A controlled treatment study of somatoform disorders including analysis of healthcare utilization and cost-effectiveness. *Journal of Psychosomatic Research, 54*, 369–380.

Hilsabeck, R. C., Gouvier, W. D., & Bolter, J. F. (1998). Reconstructive memory bias in recall of neuropsychological symptomatology. *Journal of Clinical and Experimental Neuropsychology, 20*, 328–338.

Hinkin, C. H., vanGorp, W. G., Satz, P., Marcotte, T., Durvasula, R. S., Wood, S., et al. (1996). Actual versus self-reported cognitive dysfunction in HIV-1 infection: Memory-metamemory dissociations. *Journal of Clinical and Experimental Neuropsychology, 18*, 431–443.

Hoffman, B. M., Papas, R. K., Chatkoff, D. K., & Kerns, R. D. (2007). Meta-analysis of psychological interventions for chronic low back pain. *Health Psychology, 26*, 1–9.

Iverson, G. L., & Binder, L. M. (2000). Detecting exaggeration and malingering in neuropsychological assessment. *Journal of Head Trauma Rehabilitation, 15*, 829–858.

Iverson, G. L., & McCracken, L. M. (1997). "Postconcussive" symptoms in persons with chronic pain. *Brain Injury, 11*, 783–790.

Janet, P. (1907). *The Major Symptoms of Hysteria.* New York: Macmillan.

Johnson, S. K., DeLuca, J., Diamond, B. J., & Natelson, B. H. (1996). Selective impairment of auditory processing in chronic fatigue syndrome: A comparison with multiple sclerosis and healthy controls. *Perceptual and Motor Skills, 83*, 51–62.

Johnson, S. K., DeLuca, J., Diamond, B. J., & Natelson, B. H. (1998). Memory dysfunction in fatiguing illness: Examining interference and distraction in short-term memory. *Cognitive Neuropsychiatry, 3*, 269–285.

Johnson, S. K., DeLuca, J., & Natelson, B. H. (1996a). Depression in fatiguing illness: Comparing patients with chronic fatigue syndrome, multiple sclerosis and depression. *Journal of Affective Disorders, 39*, 21–30.

Johnson, S. K., DeLuca, J., & Natelson, B. H. (1996b). Assessing somatization disorder in the chronic fatigue syndrome. *Psychosomatic Medicine, 58*, 50–57.

Johnson, S. K., DeLuca, J., & Natelson, B. H. (1996c). Personality dimensions in the chronic fatigue syndrome: A comparison with multiple sclerosis and depression. *Journal of Psychiatric Research, 30*, 9–20.

Johnson, S. K., Lange, G., Tiersky, L., DeLuca, J., & Natelson, B. H. (2001). Health-related personality variables in chronic fatigue syndrome and multiple sclerosis. *Journal of Chronic Fatigue Syndrome, 8*, 41–52.

Keefe, F. J., & Gil, K. M. (1986). Behavioral concepts in the analysis of chronic pain syndromes. *Journal of Consulting and Clinical Psychology, 54*, 776–783.

Kihlstrom, J. F. (1992). Dissociative and conversion disorders. In D. J. Stein & J. Young (Eds.), *Cognitive Science and Clinical Disorders* (pp. 247–270). San Diego, CA: Academic Press.

Kirmayer, L. J. (1996). Cultural comments on somatoform and dissociative disorders: I. In H. Fabrega, J. Mezzich, & A. Kleinman (Eds.), *Culture and*

Psychiatric Diagnosis: A DSM-IV Perspective. Washington, DC: American Psychiatric Press.

Kirmayer, L. J., Groleau, D., Looper, K. J., & Dao, M. D. (2004). Explaining medically unexplained symptoms. *Canadian Journal of Psychiatry, 49,* 663–672.

Kirmayer, L. J., & Young A. (1998). Culture and somatization: Clinical, epidemiological, and ethnographic perspectives. *Psychosomatic Medicine, 60,* 420–430.

Kleinman, A. M. (1977). Depression, somatization, and the "new cross-cultural psychiatry." *Social Science and Medicine, 11,* 3–10.

Kroenke, K., Spitzer, R. L., deGruy, F. V., 3rd, Hahn, S. R., Linzer, M., Williams, J. B., et al. (1997). Multisomatoform disorder. An alternative to undifferentiated somatoform disorder for the somatizing patient in primary care. *Archives of General Psychiatry, 54,* 352–358.

Kroenke, K., Spitzer, R. L., & Williams, J. B. W. (2002). The PHQ-15: Validity of a new measure for evaluating the severity of somatic symptoms. *Psychosomatic Medicine, 64,* 258–266.

Kroenke, K., & Swindle, R. (2000). Cognitive-behavioral therapy for somatization and symptom syndromes: A critical review of controlled clinical trials. *Psychotherapy and Psychosomatics, 69,* 205–215.

Krupp, L. B., Sliwinski, M., Masur, D. M., & Friedberg, F. (1994). Cognitive functioning and depression in patients with chronic fatigue syndrome and multiple sclerosis. *Archives of Neurology, 51,* 705–710.

Labarge, A. S., & McCaffrey, R. J. (2000). Multiple chemical sensitivity: A review of the theoretical and research literature. *Neuropsychology Review, 10,* 183–211.

Lamberg, L. (2005). New mind/body tactics target medically unexplained physical symptoms and fears. *JAMA, 294,* 2152–2154.

Lamberty, G. J., Courtney, J. C., & Heilbronner, R. L. (Eds.). (2003). *The Practice of Clinical Neuropsychology: A Survey of Practices and Settings.* Lisse, The Netherlands: Swets & Zeitlinger.

Landre, N., Poppe, C. J., Davis, N., Schmaus, B., & Hobbs, S. E. (2006). Cognitive functioning and postconcussive symptoms in trauma patients with and without mild TBI. *Archives of Clinical Neuropsychology, 21,* 255–273.

Landro, N. I., Stiles, T. C., & Sletvold, H. (1997). Memory functioning in patients with primary fibromyalgia and major depression and healthy controls. *Journal of Psychosomatic Research, 42,* 297–306.

Lane, R. D., Sechrest, L., Reidel, R., Shapiro, D. E., & Kaszniak, A. W. (2000). Pervasive emotion recognition deficit common to alexithymia and the repressive coping style. *Psychosomatic Medicine, 62,* 492–501.

Larrabee, G. J. (Ed.). (2005a). *Forensic Neuropsychology: A Scientific Approach.* New York: Oxford University Press.

Larrabee, G. J. (2005b). Assessment of malingering. In G. J. Larrabee (Ed.), *Forensic Neuropsychology: A Scientific Approach.* New York: Oxford University Press.

Larrabee, G. J. (2005c). Mild traumatic brain injury. In G. J. Larrabee (Ed.), *Forensic Neuropsychology: A Scientific Approach.* New York: Oxford University Press.

Larrabee, G. J. (2007). Evaluation of exaggerated health and injury symptomatology. In G. J. Larrabee (Ed.), Assessment of *Malingered Neuropsychological Deficits.* New York: Oxford University Press.

Larrabee, G.J, & Levin, H. (1986). Memory self-ratings and objective test performance in a normal elderly sample. *Journal of Clinical and Experimental Neuropsychology, 8,* 275–284.

Ledoux, J. (1996). *The Emotional Brain: The Mysterious Underpinnings of Emotional Life.* New York: Touchstone.

Lee, S. (1997). A chinese perspective of somatoform disorders. *Journal of Psychosomatic Research, 43,* 115–119.

Lees-Haley, P. R. (1992). Efficacy of the MMPI-2 validity scales for detecting spurious PTSD claims: F, F-K, Fake Bad Scale, Ego Strength, Subtle-Obvious subscales, DIS and DEB. *Journal of Clinical Psychology, 48,* 681–689.

Lees-Haley, P. R., English, L. T., & Glenn, W. J. (1991). A Fake Bad Scale on the MMPI-2 for personal injury claimants. *Psychological Reports, 68,* 208–210.

Lees-Haley, P. R., Iverson, G. L., Lange, R. T., Fox, D. D., & Allen, L. M. (2002). Malingering in forensic neuropsychology: Daubert and the MMPI-2. *Journal of Forensic Neuropsychology, 3,* 167–203.

Liu, G., Clark, M. R., & Eaton, W. W. (1997). Structural factor analyses for medically unexplained somatic symptoms of somatization disorder in the Epidemiologic Catchment Area study. *Psychological Medicine, 27,* 617–626.

Locke, D. E. C., Berry, D. T. R., Fakhoury, T. A., & Schmitt, F. A. (2006). Relationship of indicators of neuropathology, psychopathology, and effort to neuropsychological results in patients with epilepsy or psychogenic non-epileptic seizures. *Journal of Clinical and Experimental Neuropsychology, 28*, 325–340.

Maines, R. P. (1999). *The Technology of Orgasm: "Hysteria," the Vibrator, and Women's Sexual Satisfaction*. Baltimore, MD: Johns Hopkins University Press.

Martens, M., Donders, J., & Millis, S. R. (2001). Evaluation of invalid response sets after traumatic head injury. *Journal of Forensic Neuropsychology, 2*, 1–18.

Martin, L., Nutting, A., Macintosh, B. R., Edworthy, S. M., Butterwick, D., Cook, J. (1996). An exercise program in the treatment of fibromyalgia. *Journal of Rheumatology, 23*, 1050–1053.

Martin, R. C., Hayes, J. S., & Gouvier, W. D. (1996). Differential vulnerability between postconcussion self-report and objective malingering tests in identifying simulated mild head injury. *Journal of Clinical Neuropsychology, 18*, 265–275.

Masi, G., Favilla, L., Millepiedi, S., & Mucci, M. (2000). Somatic symptoms in children and adolescents referred for emotional and behavioral disorders. *Psychiatry, 63*, 140–149.

Matthews, C. G., Shaw, D. J., & Klove, H. (1966). Psychological test performance in neurologic and "pseudo-neurologic" subjects. *Cortex, 2*, 244–253.

Mayou, R., Bass, C., & Sharpe, M. (1995). *Treatment of Functional Somatic Symptoms*. London: Oxford University Press.

Mayou, R., Kirmayer, L. J., Simon, G., Kroenke, K., & Sharpe, M. (2005). Somatoform disorders: Time for a new approach in DSM-V. *American Journal of Psychiatry, 162*, 847–855.

McAllister, T. W. (2005). Mild brain injury and the postconcussion syndrome. In J. M. Silver, T. W. McAllister, & S. C. Yudofsky (Eds.), *Textbook of Traumatic Brain Injury* (pp. 279–308). Washington, DC: American Psychiatric Publishing.

McCrea, M., Guskiewicz, K. M., Marshall, S. W., Barr, W., Randolph, C., Cantu, R. C., et al. (2003). Acute effects and recovery time following concussion in collegiate football players: The NCAA Concussion Study. *Journal of the American Medical Association, 290*, 2556–2563.

Mealy, L. (1995). The sociobiology of sociopathy: An integrated evolutionary model. *Behavioral and Brain Sciences, 18*, 523–599.

Melville D. I. (1987). Descriptive clinical research and medically unexplained physical symptoms. *Journal of Psychosomatic Research, 31*, 359–365.

Millis, S. R., Putnam, S. H., Adams, K. M., & Ricker, J. H. (1995). The California Verbal Learning Test in detection of incomplete effort in neuropsychological evaluation. *Psychological Assessment, 7*, 463–471.

Mittenberg, W., Aguila-Puentes, G., Patton, C., Canyock, E. M., & Heilbronner, R. L. (2002). Neuropsychological profiling of symptom exaggeration and malingering. *Journal of Forensic Neuropsychology, 3*, 227–240.

Mittenberg, W., & Strauman, S. (2000). Diagnosis of mild head injury and the postconcussion syndrome. *Journal of Head Trauma Rehabilitation, 15*, 783–791.

Morey, L. C. (1991). *The Personality Assessment Inventory. Professional Manual.* Lutz, FL: Psychological Assessment Resources.

Muñoz, M., & Esteve, R. (2005). Reports of memory functioning by patients with chronic pain. *Clinical Journal of Pain, 21*, 287–291.

Nelson, N. W., Sweet, J. J., & Demakis, G. (2006). Meta-analysis of the MMPI-2 Fake Bad Scale: Utility in forensic practice. *Clinical Neuropsychologist, 20*, 39–58.

Nelson, N. W., Sweet, J. J., & Heilbronner, R. L. (2007). Examination of the new MMPI-2 Response Bias Scale (Gervais): Relationship with MMPI-2 validity scales. *Journal of Clinical and Experimental Neuropsychology, 29*, 67–72.

Nichter, M. (1981). Idioms of distress: Alternatives in the expression of psychosocial distress: A case study from South India. *Culture, Medicine and Psychiatry, 5*, 379–408.

Nimnuan, C., Rabe-Hesketh, S., Wessely S., & Hotopf, M. (2001). How many functional somatic syndromes? *Journal of Psychosomatic Research, 51*, 549–557.

Österberg, K., Orbæk, P., & Karlson, B. (2002). Neuropsychological test performance of Swedish multiple chemical sensitivity patients—an exploratory study. *Applied Neuropsychology, 9*, 139–147.

Park, D. C., Glass, J. M., Minear, M., & Crofford, L. J. (2001). Cognitive function in fibromyalgia patients. *Arthritis and Rheumatism, 44*, 2125–2133.

Pepper, C. M., Krupp, L. B., Friedberg, F., & Doscher, C. (1993). A comparison of neuropsychiatric characteristics in chronic fatigue syndrome, multiple sclerosis, and major depression. *Journal of Neuropsychiatry and Clinical Neurosciences, 5*, 200–205.

Perley, M. J., & Guze, S. B. (1962). Hysteria: The stability and usefulness of clinical criteria. *Diseases of the Nervous System, 33*, 617–621.

Phillips, K. A., First, M. B., & Pincus, H. A. (Eds.). (2003). *Advancing DSM: Dilemmas in psychiatric diagnosis.* Washington, DC: American Psychiatric Association.

Pilowsky, I., & Spence, N. D. (1983). *Manual for the illness behaviour questionnaire (IBQ).* 2nd ed. Adelaide: University of Adelaide.

Pinker, S. (1999). How the mind works. In D. C. Grossman & H. Valtin (Eds.), *Great Issues for Medicine in the Twenty-First Century: A Consideration of the Ethical and Social Issues Arising Out of Advances in the Biomedical Sciences, Sep 1997, Dartmouth Medical School, Hanover, US* (pp. 119–127). New York: New York Academy of Sciences.

Poreh, A. (2002). Neuropsychological and psychological issues associated with cross-cultural and minority assessment. In F. R. Ferraro (Ed.), *Minority and Cross-cultural Aspects of Neuropsychological Assessment* (pp. 329–343). Lisse, The Netherlands: Swets & Zeitlinger.

Raine, R., Carter, S., Sensky, T., & Black, N. (2004). General practitioners' perceptions of chronic fatigue syndrome and beliefs about its management, compared with irritable bowel syndrome: Qualitative study. *BMJ, 328*, 1354–1357.

Rao, S. M., Leo, G. J., Bernardin, L., & Unverzagt, F. (1991). Cognitive dysfunction in multiple sclerosis: I. Frequency, patterns, and prediction. *Neurology, 41*, 685–691.

Regier, D. A., Myers, J. K., Kramer M., Robins, L. N., Blazer, D. G., Hough, R. et al. (1984). The NIMH Epidemiologic Catchment Area program. Historical context, major objectives, and study population characteristics. *Archives of General Psychiatry, 41*, 934–941.

Roberts, R. J., Varney, N. R., Hulbert, J. R., & Paulsen, J. S. (1990). The neuropathology of everyday life: The frequency of partial seizure symptoms among normals. *Neuropsychology, 4*, 65–85.

Robins, L. N., & Reiger, D. A. (1991). *Psychiatric Disorders in America: The Epidemiologic Catchment Area Study.* New York: Free Press.

Robins, L. N., Helzer, J. E., Croughan, J., Ratcliff, K. S. (1981). The NIMH Diagnostic Interview Schedule, its history, characteristics, and validity. *Archives of General Psychiatry, 38*, 381–389.

Rohling, M. L., Green, P., Allen, L. M., & Iverson, G. L. (2002). Depressive symptoms and neurocognitive test scores in patients passing symptom validity tests. *Archives of Clinical Neuropsychology, 17*, 205–222.

Ross, S. R., Millis, S. R., Krukowski, R. A., Putnam, S. H., & Adams, K. M. (2004). Detecting incomplete effort on the MMPI-2: An examination of the Fake-Bad Scale in mild head injury. *Journal of Clinical and Experimental Neuropsychology, 26*, 115–124.

Rourke, S. B., Halman, M. H., & Bassel, C. (1999). Neurocognitive complaints in HIV-infection and their relationship to depressive symptoms and neuropsychological functioning. *Journal of Clinical and Experimental Neuropsychology, 21*, 737–756.

Schmidt, S., Strauss, B., & Braehler, E. (2002). Subjective physical complaints and hypochondriacal features from an attachment theoretical perspective. *Psychology and Psychotherapy: Theory, Research and Practice, 75*, 313–332.

Schore, A. N. (1994). *Affect Regulation and the Origin of the Self: The Neurobiology of Emotional Development.* Hillsdale, NJ: Lawrence Erlbaum.

Schore, A. N. (2001). The effects of early relational trauma on right brain development, affect regulation, and infant mental health. *Infant Mental Health Journal, 22*, 201–269.

Schore, A. N. (2002). Dysregulation of the right brain: A fundamental mechanism of traumatic attachment and the psychopathogenesis of posttraumatic stress disorder. *Australian and New Zealand Journal of Psychiatry, 36*, 9–30.

Schretlen, D. J., & Shapiro, A. M. (2003). A quantitative review of the effects of traumatic brain injury on cognitive functioning. *International Review of Psychiatry, 15*, 341–349.

Severens, J. L., Prins, I. B., van der Wilt, G. J., van der Meer, J. W. M., & Bleijenberg, G. (2004). Cost-effectiveness of cognitive behaviour therapy for patients with chronic fatigue syndrome. *QJM: An International Journal of Medicine, 97*, 153–161.

Shapiro, D. (1965). *Neurotic Styles.* New York: Basic Books.

Sharpe, M., & Carson, A. (2001). "Unexplained" somatic symptoms, functional syndromes, and somatization: Do we need a paradigm shift? *Annals of Internal Medicine, 134*, 926–930.

Shorter, E. (1992). *From Paralysis to Fatigue: A History of Psychosomatic Illness in the Modern Era.* New York: Free Press.

Sifneos, P. E. (1987). *Short-Term Dynamic Psychotherapy: Evaluation and Technique*, 2nd ed. New York: Plenum Press.

Simon, G. E., Daniell, W., Stockbridge, H., Claypoole, K., & Rosenstock, L. (1993). Immunologic, psychological, and neuropsychological factors in multiple chemical sensitivity. A controlled study. *Annals of Internal Medicine, 119*, 97–103.

Simon, G. E., & Gureje, O. (1999). Stability of somatization disorder and somatization symptoms among primary care patients. *Archives of General Psychiatry, 156*, 90–95.

Sjodin, I., Svedlund, J., Ottosson, J., & Dotevall, G. (1986). Controlled study of psychotherapy in chronic peptic ulcer disease. *Psychosomatics: Journal of Consultation Liaison Psychiatry, 27*, 187–200.

Slavney, P. R., & Teitelbaum, M. L. (1985). Patients with medically unexplained symptoms: *DSM-III* diagnoses and demographic characteristics. *General Hospital Psychiatry, 7*, 21–25.

Smith, R. C., Gardiner, J. C., Lyles, J. S., Sirbu, C., Dwamena, F. C., Hodges, A., et al. (2006). Exploration of DSM-IV criteria in primary care patients with medically unexplained symptoms, *Psychosomatic Medicine, 67*, 123–129.

Spitzer, R. L., Williams, J. B., & Kroenke, K. (1994). Utility of a new procedure for diagnosing mental disorders in primary care. The PRIME-MD 1000 study. *JAMA, 272*, 1749–1756.

Stanos, S. P., McLean, J., & Rader, L. (2007). Physical medicine rehabilitation approach to pain. *Medical Clinics of North America, 91*, 57–95.

Staudenmayer, H., & Phillips, S. (2007). MMPI-2 validity, clinical and content scales, and the Fake Bad Scale for personal injury litigants claiming idiopathic environmental intolerance. *Journal of Psychosomatic Research, 62*, 61–72.

Stewart, A. L., Hays, R. D., & Ware, J. E. (1988). The MOS Short form general health survey: Reliability and validity in a patient population. *Medical Care, 26*, 724–735.

Stone, J., Wojcik, W., Durrance, D., Carson, A., Lewis, S., & MacKenzie, L. et al. (2002). What should we say to patients with symptoms unexplained by disease? The "number needed to offend." *BMJ: British Medical Journal, 325,* 1449–1450.

Stuart, S. (2006). Interpersonal psychotherapy: A guide to the basics. *Psychiatric Annals, 36,* 542–550.

Stuart, S., & Noyes, R. (2006). Interpersonal psychotherapy for somatizing patients. *Psychotherapy and Psychosomatics, 75,* 209–219.

Suhr, J. (2003). Neuropsychological impairment in fibromyalgia: Relation to depression, fatigue, and pain. *Journal of Psychosomatic Research, 55,* 321–329.

Suhr, J., Tranel, D., Wefel, J., & Barrash, J. (1997). Memory performance after head injury: Contributions of malingering, litigation status, psychological factors, and medication use. *Journal of Clinical and Experimental Neuropsychology, 19,* 500–514.

Sumanti, M., Boone, K. B., Savodnik, I., & Gorsuch, R. (2006). Noncredible psychiatric and cognitive symptoms and a worker's compensation "stress" claims sample. *Clinical Neuropsychologist, 20,* 754–765.

Sumathipala, A., Hewege, R., Hanwella, R., & Mann, A. H. (2000). Randomized controlled trial of cognitive behaviour therapy for repeated consultations for medically unexplained complaints: A feasibility study in Sri Lanka. *Psychological Medicine, 30,* 747–757.

Svedlund, J. (1983). Psychotherapy in irritable bowel syndrome: A controlled outcome study. *Acta Psychiatrica Scandinavica, 67,* 7–86.

Svedlund, J., Sjodin, I., Ottosson, J. O., & Dotevall, G. (1983). Controlled study of psychotherapy in irritable bowel syndrome. *Lancet, 2,* 589–592.

Sweet, J. (Ed.). (1999). *Forensic Neuropsychology: Fundamentals and Practice.* Lisse, The Netherlands: Swets & Zeitlinger.

Sweet, J. J., Nelson, N. W., & Moberg, P. J. (2006). The TCN/AACN 2005 "salary survey": Professional practices, beliefs, and incomes of U.S. neuropsychologists. *Clinical Neuropsychologist, 20,* 325–364.

Sweet, J. J., Peck, E. A. I., Abramowitz, C., & Etzweiler, S. (2002). National Academy of Neuropsychology/Division 40 of the American Psychological Association practice survey of clinical neuropsychology in the United States, part I: Practitioner and practice characteristics, professional activities, and time requirements. *Clinical Neuropsychologist, 16,* 109–127.

Taillefer, S. S., Kirmayer, L. J., Robbins, J. M., & Lasry, J. (2002). Psychological correlates of functional status in chronic fatigue syndrome. *Journal of Psychosomatic Research, 53*, 1097–1106.

Taillefer, S. S., Kirmayer, L. J., Robbins, J. M., & Lasry, J. (2003). Correlates of illness worry in chronic fatigue syndrome. *Journal of Psychosomatic Research, 54*, 331–337.

Taylor, G. J., Bagby, R. M., & Parker, J. D. A. (1997). *Disorders of Affect Regulation: Alexithymia in Medical and Psychiatric Illness*. New York: Cambridge University Press.

Taylor, S., & Asmundson, G. J. G. (2004). *Treating Health Anxiety: A Cognitive-Behavioral Approach*. New York: Guilford Press.

Tazaki, M., & Landlaw, K. (2006). Behavioural mechanisms and cognitive-behavioural interventions of somatoform disorders. *International Review of Psychiatry. Special Issue: Somatoform Disorders, 18*, 67–73.

Tiersky, L. A., Johnson, S. K., Lange, G., Natelson, B. H., & DeLuca, J. (1997). Neuropsychology of chronic fatigue syndrome: A critical review. *Journal of Clinical and Experimental Neuropsychology, 19*, 560–586.

Tombaugh, T. N. (1996). *TOMM. Test of Memory Malingering*. Tonawanda, NY: Multi-Health Systems, Inc.

Trimble, M. (2004). *Somatoform Disorders: A Medicolegal Guide*. Cambridge: Cambridge University Press.

Turk, D. C., Meichenbaum, D. H., & Genest, M. (1983). *Pain and Behavioral Medicine: A Cognitive-Behavioral Perspective*. New York: Guilford Press.

van der Werf, S. P., Prins, J. B., Jongen, P. J. H., van der Meer, J. W. M., & Bleijenberg, G. (2000). Abnormal neuropsychological findings are not necessarily a sign of cerebral impairment: A matched comparison between chronic fatigue syndrome and multiple sclerosis. *Neuropsychiatry, Neuropsychology, and Behavioral Neurology, 13*, 199–203.

Van Houdenhove, B., Neerinckx, E., Onghena, P., Vingerhoets, A., Lysens, R., & Vertommen, H. (2002). Daily hassles reported by chronic fatigue syndrome and fibromyalgia patients in tertiary care: A controlled quantitative and qualitative study. *Psychotherapy and Psychosomatics, 71*, 207–213.

Vermeulen, J., Aldenkamp, A. P., & Alpherts, W. C. (1993). Memory complaints in epilepsy: Correlations with cognitive performance and neuroticism. *Epilepsy Research, 15*, 157–170.

Wagner, M. T., Wymer, J. H., Topping, K. B., & Pritchard, P. B. (2005). Use of the Personality Assessment Inventory as an efficacious and cost-effective diagnostic tool for nonepileptic seizures. *Epilepsy and Behavior, 7*, 301–304.

Waldinger, R. J., Schulz, M. S., Barsky, A. J., & Ahern, D. K. (2006). Mapping the road from childhood trauma to adult somatization: The role of attachment. *Psychosomatic Medicine, 68*, 129–135.

Waller, E., & Scheidt, C. E. (2006). Somatoform disorders as disorders of affect regulation: A development perspective. *International Review of Psychiatry, 18*, 13–24.

Wang, Y., Chan, R. C., & Deng, Y. (2006). Examination of postconcussion-like symptoms in healthy university students: Relationships to subjective and objective neuropsychological function performance. *Archives of Clinical Neuropsychology, 21*, 339–347.

Ware, J. J., & Sherbourne, C. D. (1992). The MOS 36-item short-form health survey (SF-36). I. Conceptual framework and item selection. *Medical Care, 30*, 473–483.

Wearden, A., Cook, L., & Vaughan-Jones, J. (2003). Adult attachment, alexithymia, symptom reporting, and health-related coping. *Journal of Psychosomatic Research, 55*, 341–347.

Wearden, A. J., Lamberton, N., Crook, N., & Walsh, V. (2005). Adult attachment, alexithymia, and symptom reporting: An extension to the four category model of attachment. *Journal of Psychosomatic Research, 58*, 279–288.

Wearden, A. J., Morris, R. K., Mullis, R., Strickland, P. L., Pearson, D. J., Appleby, L., Campbell, I. T., Morris, J. A. (1998). Randomized, double-blind, placebo-controlled treatment trial of fluoxetine and graded exercise for chronic fatigue syndrome. *British Journal of Psychiatry, 172*, 485–490.

Weiss, E., & Spurgeon, O. (1943). *Psychosomatic Medicine: The Clinical Application of Psychopathology to General Medical Problems.* Philadelphia: W. B. Saunders Company.

Wessely, S., Nimnuan, C., & Sharpe, M. (1999). Functional somatic syndromes: One or many? *Lancet, 354*, 936–939.

Whorwell, P. J., Prior, A., & Farragher, E. B. (1984). Controlled trial of hypnotherapy in the treatment of severe refractory irritable bowel syndrome. *Lancet, 2*, 1232–1234.Wilkus, R.J., Dodrill, C.B., & Thompson, P.M. (1984). Intensive EEG monitoring and psychological studies of patients with pseudoepileptic seizures. *Epilepsia, 25*, 100–107.

Williams, L., & Day, A. (2007). Strategies for dealing with clients we dislike. *American Journal of Family Therapy, 35*, 83–92.

Wilson, R. S., Arnold, S. E., Schneider, J. A., Li, Y., & Bennett, D. A. (2007). Chronic distress, age-related neuropathology, and late-life dementia. *Psychosomatic Medicine, 69*, 47–53.

Wittchen, H. U., Robins, L. N., Cottler, L. B., Sartorius, N., Burke, J. D., & Regier, D. (1991). Cross-cultural feasibility, reliability and sources of variance of the Composite International Diagnostic Interview (CIDI). The Multicentre WHO/ADAMHA Field Trials. *British Journal of Psychiatry, 159*, 645–653.

Wolfe, F., Ross, K., Anderson, J., Russell, I. J., & Hebert, L. (1995). The prevalence and characteristics of fibromyalgia in the general population. *Arthritis and Rheumatism, 38*, 19–28.

Wong, T. M. (2006). Ethical controversies in neuropsychological test selection, administration, and interpretation. *Applied Neuropsychology, 13*, 68–76.

Wood, J. N., Romero, S. G., Knutson, K. M., & Grafman, J. (2005). Representation of attitudinal knowledge: Role of prefrontal cortex, amygdala and parahippocampal gyrus. *Neuropsychologia, 43*, 249–259.

Woolfolk, R. L., & Allen, L. A. (2007). *Treating Somatization: A Cognitive-Behavioral Approach.* New York: Guilford Press.

World Health Organization. (1992). *International Statistical Classification of Diseases and Related Health Problems*, 10th rev. Geneva: Author.

World Health Organization. (1998). *SCAN: Schedules for Clinical Assessment in Neuropsychiatry*, version 2.1. Geneva: WHO Division of Mental Health.

Index

abridged somatization, 15, 24
ACBT. *See* affective cognitive behavior therapy
acculturation, 46
affective cognitive behavior therapy (ACBT), 77–78
affect regulation, 40, 43
alexithymia, 43
Allen, L.A., 77, 101
American Psychosomatic Society, 69
Anna O., 38
anxiety disorders, 10, 17, 18
attachment theory, 39–44, 75
autoimmune disorders, 63–66

Beck Depression Inventory, 54
behaviorally oriented theories, 35–37
biases, 67–68, 97, 101
biologically oriented theories, 32–35
bipolar affective disorder, 31
Bowlby, John, 39, 40
brain, 34, 43, 67
breast cancer, 48
Breuer, Josef, 37, 38
Briquet, Paul, 5
Briquet's syndrome, 5

CBT. *See* cognitive behavior therapy
CFS. *See* chronic fatigue syndrome
Charcot, Jean-Martin, 5, 6
chemotherapy, 48
children
    attachment theory, 39–44
    pediatric somatization, 27–28
    trauma of, 42
chronic distress, 48
chronic fatigue syndrome (CFS), 14, 16, 34, 55, 56–57, 64, 71, 72, 73, 74
chronic pain, 56–57
chronic symptoms, 13

clinical interview, 91–94
cognitive behavior therapy (CBT), 70, 71–74, 76
    See also affective cognitive behavior therapy
cognitive dysfunction, 47–50
Composite International Diagnostic Interview, 24
consciousness, 69
consultation liaison psychiatry, 69
conversion, 6, 17, 37–38, 96, 97
culture-bound syndromes, 44
cultures, 18, 44–46, 103

Damasio, Antonio R., 69
Darwin, Charles, 34, 39
depression, 18, 23, 31
Descartes, René, 69
Descartes' Error (Damasio), 69
diabetes, 48
diagnoses
    alternatives to current criteria, 15–16
    of neuropsychologists, 101
    new approach to, 16–19
    psychiatric, 9–10, 25, 29, 44
    somatization disorder, 15
    somatoform, 13–15
Diagnostic and Statistical Manual of Mental Disorders-III, 5, 10, 11, 13–15, 22, 23, 29, 31
Diagnostic and Statistical Manual of Mental Disorders-IV, 10–13, 17–19, 21–25, 29, 38, 44, 52
disability, 52
dissociation, 37, 42
distress, 48–49, 54, 97

ECA. *See* National Institutes of Mental Health Epidemiologic Catchment Area (ECA) study

natural selection, 34
nature/nurture issue, 39
"nervous" conditions, 4, 5, 59
nervous system, 4, 34
NESs. See nonepileptic seizures
neurology, 5, 25–27, 29
neuropsychological assessment, 47–66
neuropsychological evaluation, 94–96
neuropsychologists, 91, 97, 101–2
neuropsychology, 69
neuroscience, 69
Nonepileptic Seizure Organization, 34
nonepileptic seizures (NESs), 54, 55,
    59–62, 90
norepinephrine, 31
nosology, 9–19

operant conditioning, 35–36

pain, 35–36, 54, 56–57, 69
paralysis, 3
pathology, 10
PCS. See postconcussive syndrome
pediatric somatization, 27–28
perceptions, 37
Persian Gulf War-related illnesses, 55
personal injury, 52
Personality Assessment Inventory, 54
pollution, 45
Portland Digit Recognition Test, 60
postconcussive syndrome (PCS), 14, 36,
    49, 62–63
posttraumatic stress syndrome, 43
preevaluation, 89–91
prevalence, 21
primary care studies, 23–25, 29
pseudoneurological illness, 55
psychiatric diagnosis, 9–10, 25, 29, 44
psychoanalytically oriented theories,
    37–39
Psychoanalytic Theory of Neurosis, The
    (Fenichel), 33
psychodynamic approaches, 10, 70,
    74–76
psychogenic seizures, 60
psychological disturbance, 50–55
psychometrists, 94–95
psychopathology, 39

psychosomatic disturbances, 33
psychosomatic medicine, 68–70
psychotherapy, 67, 68, 69, 71, 76–77,
    100, 101

RBS. See Response Bias Scale
Renaissance, 4
Response Bias Scale (RBS), 53–54
Revised Symptom Checklist 90, 54
right hemisphere, 43

Schedules for Clinical Assessment in
    Neuropsychiatry, 26
schizophrenia, 10, 23, 31
secondary gain, 51
secure attachment, 40
sensory information, 37
serotonin, 31
Shorter, Edward, 3–4, 6
Short Form General Health Survey, 24
sick building syndrome, 16, 55
silicone breast implant illness, 55
somatic stress disorders, 55
somatization disorder
    cognitive dysfunction in, 47–50
    cultural issues in, 44–46, 103
    definition of, 11
    developmental theories of, 39–44, 70
    disorders/syndromes associated with,
        55–66
    in DSM-III, 10, 13, 14
    in DSM-IV, 5, 11, 12
    evolutionary psychological approach
        to, 35
    future of treatment for, 78–79
    and neuropsychological symptoms,
        47–55
    pediatric, 27–28
    psychological disturbance in, 50–55
    symptoms of, 6, 11–14, 17, 31, 71
    terminology, 14, 37, 38, 96
somatizing patients, 14, 81–103
    clinical interview, 91–94
    evaluation report, 96–99
    expressive pattern, 81, 84–89, 91–92
    feedback sessions, 99–101
    neuropsychological evaluation, 94–96
    preevaluation, 89–91

somatizing patients (*continued*)
  presentation of, 81–88
  referral for services, 101–3
  stoic pattern, 81–84, 88–89, 91,
    92–93
somatoform disorders
  and attachment theory, 40
  behaviorally oriented theories of,
    35–37
  biologically oriented theories of,
    32–35
  cognitive behavior therapy
    approaches, 71–74, 76
  and *DSM-IV*, 10–13, 29
  epidemiology of, 21–29
  etiological theories of, 31–46
  history of, 3–7
  management of, 67–79
  and neuropsychological assessment,
    47–66
  nosology of, 9–19
  psychoanalytically oriented theories
    of, 37–39
  psychodynamic approaches, 74–76
  symptoms of, 3–7, 17, 18, 29,
    31–32
  treatment literature on, 71
somatoform pain disorder, 14
somatoform syndromes, 14
spas, 5
spinal reflexes, 4
Stekel, Wilhelm, 37
stoic patients, 81–84, 88–89, 91,
  92–93
strange situation procedure, 40
stress idiom, 45

Studies on Hysteria (Breuer and Freud),
  38
SVTs. *See* symptom validity tests
Sydenham, Thomas, 4, 5
Symptom Checklist, 26
symptoms
  chronic, 13
  functional somatic, 34, 78–79
  medically unexplained, 14, 15,
    23–26, 48, 55
  "nervous," 59
  of somatization disorder, 6, 11–14,
    17, 31, 71
  of somatoform disorders, 3–7, 17, 18,
    29, 31–32
  unexplained, 13
symptom validity tests (SVTs), 46

testing, 94–96
Test of Memory Malingering, 46, 57
toxic mold, 55
trauma, 6, 37, 42–44, 45, 74
Treating Somatization (Woolfolk and
  Allen), 77
Treatment of Functional Somatic Symptoms
  (Mayou et al.), 78

unconscious conflicts, 38
unexplained symptoms, 13

wandering uterus, 3, 32–33, 34
Whiteley Index, 26
Whytt, Robert, 4
women, 3–4, 22, 35
Woolfolk, R.L., 77, 101
Word Memory Test, 46

About the Author

Greg J. Lamberty, Ph.D. is a clinical neuropsychologist with the Noran Neurological Clinic in Minneapolis, MN and an adjunct Professor at the University of St. Thomas in the Graduate School of Professional Psychology. He has also held adjunct faculty positions at the University of Iowa and Purdue University. Dr. Lamberty has served on the Board of Directors of the American Academy of Clinical Neuropsychology (AACN) since 2002 and was the original Annual Meeting Committee chairperson. He served as the Program Chair for the AACN Annual Meeting and Workshops inaugural meeting in 2003 through the 2007 meeting. Dr. Lamberty is a consulting editor for the *Journal of Clinical and Experimental Neuropsychology* and has been active in a range of practice related activities in his profession. He co-edited *The Practice of Clinical Neuropsychology* (2003) and has served on a number of scientific and practice related committees through the American Psychological Association, The Midwest Neuropsychology Group, the International Neuropsychological Society, and the Indiana Psychological Association.

Lightning Source UK Ltd.
Milton Keynes UK
171161UK00004B/92/P

9 780195 328271